Dan

You might recognise some
of the ramblings + musings
from my time at SPHS!
I had to write something to
try to make sense of it all.
At least I have had a go!
Thanks for all your support
and camaraderie over the
many years. Hope you enjoy
the rest of your career as much
as I have enjoyed (most) of mine!

Pete.

June 2015

Walls and Bridges

Building a picture of human nature

By Peter McMahon

Honeybee Books

Published by Honeybee Books
Broadoak, Dorset
www.honeybeebooks.co.uk

Printed in the UK using paper from sustainable sources

ISBN: 978-1-910616-27-7
Contact the author at PMcMahon@sphs.uk.com

Contents

Introduction

As I start to write this brief background to introduce my theme, another academic year has just drawn to a close and the summer lies ahead. I plan to end my teaching career, currently spanning 20 years, at the end of the next academic year 2014-2015. Teaching has been the latter part of my working life. Previously I have worked in the Aerospace and Construction industries, the Department for Employment at various different levels and in Advertising and Recruitment. Originally I might well have left my present education employer at 60, but the politicians, among others, thought otherwise and so I decided to stay on for two more years on a part-time contract. It was-and still is-my hope to use any perceived expertise, together with some of the extra hours, to be a much better teacher (or "reflective practitioner" if you want the proper jargon) and to be able to pass on some of my hard-won experience to younger colleagues, especially those setting out in teaching today. You would have to ask them whether or not I have been successful but I certainly have tried.

The last twenty years have seen me teaching Religious Education including "A"-Level Philosophy, Theology and Ethics at a large Catholic Secondary school in the South West of England. I have always enjoyed the interaction with the students and have endeavoured to deliver my subject with passion and care. It is a very hard subject to teach well if students are to be properly challenged in their faith but also to be properly respected at their stage on the journey.

It was a few years ago whilst teaching a module to Year 9 (14 year-olds) on the topics of Conflict and Reconciliation, a really detailed and thorough module planned to take a good portion of the autumn school term, that I started fully to understand what really characterised human nature. Of course I knew many of the basics before that, but with age our reflective ability matures, the questions and challenges provided by many of my students causing me to think around the issues in quite some depth. As a teacher of Religious Education I am well used to using symbolism to aid understanding. That module was in two distinct but interrelated parts. Firstly, the nature of conflict in all its forms and secondly the value of reconciliation in the many ways it has been attempted with greater or lesser success throughout history.

It became apparent to me that two types of construction, namely walls and bridges, had much to offer as symbols in helping students to understand what we as human beings have built up and destroyed and in many cases re-built, not only physically but also intellectually, emotionally and spiritually in society. I felt that this would help me teach the conflict and reconciliation module better. On searching the internet for information on these resources, I have found, as you might expect, plenty of examples of the many physical structures around the planet of both types, interestingly with far more books written discretely about bridges than walls. Dan Cruickshank's "Bridges-Heroic Designs that Changed the World" (Collins, 2010), for example, gives an excellent historical and cultural perspective to innovative bridge design. A few works touched on the deeper symbolic aspects of bridges.

Dipping in, I began to get a lot more clued up on some of those bridges about which I knew little or nothing, as well as finding out more about those well-known constructions which you would no doubt be expecting me to mention in the coming chapters. What I struggled to find anywhere, though, was any existing work that dealt with the both types of construction, walls and bridges, from a combination of both physical and symbolic perspectives. I decided, therefore, to rectify this by selecting and discussing a few of each which I hope you will agree have significance and an interest factor and which I contend shed some light on our nature as human beings.

In fact, when I mentioned that I was planning to write a book on this broader topic, I received a steady trickle of suggestions, for which I am very grateful, although my plan would certainly not leave room to include them all! Furthermore, the last thing I would wish is to burden anyone with a book which it would be totally impractical to read!

Former Beatle John Lennon wrote an album entitled Walls and Bridges, released in 1974, during his separation from Yoko Ono and his move to California with their personal assistant May Pang. A mixture of album tracks suggests a variety of themes ranging from the loss of Ono to his fear of ageing, loneliness and the emptiness of success together with some disillusionment about show business. Lennon was obviously concerned about the barriers between himself and others especially in his relationships and his hopes that those barriers could be overcome. As there are no specific walls or bridges highlighted, perhaps he was intending to work through the barriers causing him to build walls in his own mind but also to think about the way forward in a different land, maybe allowing him some objectivity and a different perspective even from breathing different air.

Many years ago, during the 1950s, my father taught in some quite challenging schools in Leeds. Having encountered learning barriers of his own and partly   in response to those barriers he wrote and published a book about making and playing marionettes. It struck me that here he was using a great resource: string puppets constructed under his expert eye and guidance by his students and played in a school theatre custom-built for the purpose. This was fairly radical although there had been a "sharp revival of interest at the time in puppets and puppet theatres" as he comments. As a skilled teaching practitioner whose talents I considered immense, Dad was not merely using an interactive resource contemporary to that generation of children, but also teaching them the social skills of teamwork and co-operation which all teachers will know to be one of the best antidotes to low self-esteem, a major problem in society then and now. Sadly, as we know to our cost, some of those with the lowest self-esteem in society can become its most reclusive and dangerous members and we all know where that can lead.

I know from a very enjoyable visit to the theatre at his school, when I was very young, that he had achieved much success in breaking down some of the walls to learning which many of his students has built in their minds. This was achieved not only by students making the marionettes, but also getting them to perform or play them in teams and with the realisation for many that

"a quick, wide-ranging intelligence is as worth acquiring as nimble fingers and capable hands"

This thought currently seems to be making a comeback in education as our politicians realise that education (from the Latin word "educere" meaning to draw out) is as much about personal skills and qualities as it is about knowledge and understanding. Social skills of patience, resilience and teamwork are surely just as vital now as they ever were then in situations where people are often asked to work collaboratively towards goals or targets.

Dad summed it up neatly:

"I believe that the children took this prevailing spirit of teamwork with them when they left school to go into workshops, factories and offices".

I hope therefore in these pages of mine to explore and to integrate the two concepts, firstly physical walls and bridges taken as structures in themselves and secondly the light that these and other more symbolic structures might shed on humans as individual and social beings. Any such insight would need of course to include some of the more negative aspects of human nature (including sadly some of the darkest days of history) but equally these would be balanced by some of the more positive ones (the tone I hope to leave at the end of my book). I intend to weave the chosen walls and bridges into each chapter, trying to include, from among many possible examples, those about which I have learned something interesting or important or which for a variety of reasons are purely some of my favourites. I trust you will grant me the liberty to do this.

I joked with one or two colleagues that this was really just an excuse to spend some of my retirement travelling the world as I would of course need to see some of the constructions first hand if I had not seen them already. However the list for both is extensive (unlike the travel budget) so I shall fit in what I can in the years I have left.

Chapter 1   Individual and Team

"One single gesture transforms nature and gives it order"
Santiago Calatrava (Architect)

At school, both as a student and latterly as a teacher, I used to love lessons on teamwork, especially the one in which we or the students were asked to construct (in small teams of say five or six individuals) either a tower or a bridge using resources which required imaginative and creative approaches to complete the task. At the end of the lesson there would normally be some kind of evaluation of the construction in terms of its functionality and perhaps its aesthetic beauty. I recall structures of all types being tested to see whether they would fall over or collapse under their own weight. Some ingenious students would inevitably try to stick with tape or even worse to glue the object to their table for extra rigidity and stability!

The key learning point was normally revealed in an ensuing discussion about the individual roles within the team (I shall refer later to team roles as put forward by psychologist Meredith Belbin) and how the team had planned and organised the building of someone's vision for the final product-or not! This was new to some students who had not previously considered that anyone might have formally identified set roles within teams or analysed their characteristics.

The best constructions were intelligently designed but practical, rigid and certainly durable until at least lunchtime when the room had to be tidied up for lessons in the afternoon. Occasionally I would keep a good one and perhaps marvel slightly at some well-disciplined team's effort to meet all the parameters of the brief including that important ability to deliver the finished project on time. I think back to this when considering bridges as one of my two chosen symbols for revealing something of our human nature.

However you define the concept of a bridge (that "single gesture transforming nature and giving it order" as Calatrava proposes), your definition is more than likely to include the idea of a structure which affords stability, support or connection whether it is over a road or river, over your nose, over your teeth, over the hull of a ship or under the strings of an instrument!

If I asked you to name the most popular, most visited or most interesting bridges around the planet, I am sure you would list of some of the following among your favourites: - The Golden Gate in San Francisco, Tower Bridge in London, Sydney Harbour Bridge, Brooklyn Bridge in New York, the Rialto and Ponte Vecchio in Venice and Florence respectively and the Charles Bridge in Prague. However, you probably know of many others, some of which might be memorable for you. I live in Gloucestershire but on a regional basis I would personally have to include a few of my favourites as Pulteney Bridge and the Palladian Bridge in Bath, Brunel's suspension bridge at Clifton, Bristol and the Tamar bridge at Plymouth. They are not necessarily among my favourites on the basis of construction only, but also on the basis of significant memories and emotions generated whenever I see them.

There are many countries in which the kudos of holding records must surely be a motivation to the continued building programmes being planned there. Records really matter to some. The bragging rights to hold the current record for the oldest, longest, shortest, widest, highest or narrowest bridge on the planet are for some architects and engineers part of their raison d'être. China apparently holds more than half of the top 10 in significant categories. Of course, there are going to be disputes and disagreements about which is indeed the oldest, longest, shortest, widest or narrowest and for how long before someone beats that record. Even as I write, the bridges I mention below may have lost their status as record holder in the name of technological advancement and I make no apology for any inaccuracies here on that account.

A fairly well-attested claim for the oldest working bridge in the world comes from a single arch stone construction over the River Meles in Izmir, Turkey. This bridge has allegedly been in use for around 2800 years. According to legends, Homer the Greek poet and even the Apostle Paul, one of the great travellers, who must have crossed many bridges on his journeys, may well have crossed over the river on this one, Paul perhaps on one of his missions to the early Christian Churches.

For the longest bridge, many point to the Danyang-Kunshan Grand

Bridge in Nanjing, Shanghai which runs broadly parallel to the Yangtze river which is some 164 kilometres long. In that delta is a mixture of canals, rivers, lakes and rice fields. Effectively a viaduct on the main Beijing-Shanghai railway system, it reputedly took around 10,000 personnel from 2006 about four years to construct. There will of course always be disagreements about how the length of a bridge is actually measured. Some argue for a shoreline to shoreline approach while others are happier with front of entrance section to end of exit section for greater accuracy.

The St. Lawrence River between New York and Ontario has an archipelago known as Thousand Islands, although there are over 1800 near this north-eastern part of Lake Ontario in Canada. Some of these islands are so small as to support only one building. The shortest bridge is regarded by many as an international boundary between two of these small islands at Zavikon and crosses the US/Canadian border although the span of the bridge is only about 32 feet. Some argue however that both islands are actually in Canada and so it should not be regarded as a border crossing.

If you are looking for wide bridges, the Bay Bridge connecting the East side of San Francisco with the West side of Oakland is arguably as wide as it gets at 17.5 metres wide in 5 lanes westbound. It is a toll bridge and opened just shortly before the much-visited Golden Gate. Connecting Oakland with San Francisco was deemed important if San Francisco was to prosper from the California gold rush of 1848-55. Without the Bay Bridge, it was deemed to be on the wrong side of the water to be a major centre for trade.

For sheer height, the Sidu River Bridge in Hubei, China boasts (according to who has measured it and from which point) about 500 metres of clearance to the gorge of the Sidu River below. It has been normal construction practice in China to use a helicopter or a boat to carry the very first bridge cable, but in the case of the Sidu bridge it was fired over the gorge by rocket, saving a great deal of time and effort. There are over 16,000 individual wires strung together in each of the main bridge cables.

Conversely if it is narrow bridges you wish to debate, Nutty Narrows in Longview, Washington is a thin aluminium pipe covered with a fire hose designed to look like a suspension bridge. This narrowest of nutty bridges was built in 1963 to allow squirrels to cross a busy thoroughfare safely, though the bridge has been moved on a couple of occasions to avoid it being a hazard to traffic. Other similar bridges have been, and will continue to be erected annually in the vicinity so it has obviously been of help to one particularly small community!

I suppose all these bridges were put together by teams. It is quite feasible, of course, for one person to build a bridge entirely on their own from concept to reality and I expect some have, and yet a project of any magnitude would surely call for a range of different skills together with a substantial increase in person-power if the project were to be finished before any one individual might need to call a halt for reasons of exhaustion or old age!

Some of the most famous bridges and obviously those in more challenging locations or where size is paramount have needed large teams of designers and builders. That Golden Gate in San Francisco with its iconic orangey colour was built by around 10 different prime contractors together with their sub -contractors. A full list of employees who worked on the bridge, something I would have loved to peruse, is sadly unavailable since the prime contractors no longer exist. We can only surmise that there was a host of engineers involved.

Going back to our bridge building activities at school, I can fully appreciate the value of team roles as described by Belbin. Without going into an exhaustive explanation of his observations, suffice it to say that a variety of roles is surely needed in any viable team working on a larger project such as a major bridge.

One story I heard a few years ago from a pair of Industrial Psychologists, with whom I used to work, involved an exercise they had been asked to undertake with a talented but misfiring team of research and development staff in a large engineering PLC along the M4 corridor. Projects were apparently late on a regular basis which was costing money and credibility even though the ideas and product quality were fantastic.

It came to light that most of the brilliantly talented engineers producing the ideas using their very fertile imaginations were near enough all First Class Honours Graduates with PhDs. Unfortunately they were of too similar a mould, and would probably be described in some versions of Belbin's team roles as fertile "plants". What they were really short of were "shapers" and "drivers" to push the projects beyond great engineering ideas into deadline-hitting realities.

Moreover, not only were shapers and drivers missing but there was also a significant lack of "resource investigators", people who could challenge the constraints on how to build the products differently or better and "monitor-evaluators" who could slow down the shapers and drivers from their relentless charging ahead with some sensible questions like "Have you considered that if you go down that route you will not be able to.."? As a result, much better balanced teams were formed by the relatively simple addition of some individuals with the requisite mind sets and skills bases.

The best teams need leaders though. Whilst some teams certainly seem to be able to function at a collegiate or co-operative level, there is still some need of a leader or leadership group to point the way. Surely this is true of most of the very best orchestras, golf teams, hospitals, armies, governments, choirs and so on. As for the style and structure of leadership, that is far more controversial.

I have known instances where two people were supposedly running a team jointly. Possibly a workable situation as long as you are absolutely in tune and yet even then what if one gets ill or has a change of personal philosophy? Can two different people always agree on everything? I have my doubts. Some great duos of the music world have gone their separate ways, having fallen out over a possible change of direction in order to keep their music fresh.

One extreme is the dictatorial leadership style which says we do things my way or else! Leaders of this type insist that if you do not like what they believe in you can go elsewhere. I fully agree with the requirement for one person to be the team's figurehead and ultimately responsible and yet for me there are many possible styles, all of which, with a little consultation, can work as far as I am concerned. In sharp contrast to the dictator surrounded by an "inner sanctum" of trusted stalwarts, all of whom can be relied upon not to confront or contradict the leader, is the relaxed and almost congenial leader who is so pleasant and seemingly caring and such a good listener that you would only wish to please them and would almost shed blood for them simply because they are just so nice to work for.

I have worked for both types (and many others in between) and would conclude that both have their strengths and weaknesses. In fact the leadership styles I have observed in my own career have been quite fascinating. One of my first bosses was Reg Gillett, a Birmingham-born Export Manager. He was a highly intelligent though quite brusque sort of character. In those days we used a lot of catch phrases and he too used plenty of these. One of his favourites was that he did not "suffer fools gladly" which basically meant you had to think before speaking to him or else! Later on I put a sign up in my classroom which read "Engage brain before opening mouth". I used to point certain students towards it at times. My goodness, how some of them needed it! Reg would have appreciated this and laughed.

Reg also taught me that no-one will blow your own trumpet for you, and so it is important to communicate effectively and let people know what is going on and especially what is going well for you at work. Another gem was his advice about those Monday morning blues. Len worked in Administration and always seemed impossible to get through to on a Monday morning. Gillett the guru taught me that communication would be virtually impossible unless I got onto Len's wavelength. To do this I had to find something he enjoyed, though which I probably didn't, but about which I could talk intelligently enough to be convincing. Horse racing was the answer to the question. Not my favourite sport, but nevertheless after doing my homework I suddenly succeeded in getting at least somewhere with Len on a Monday when previously it had been the stone wall treatment! Nice advice Reg!

One of the best I worked for was Wilf Styles. He was a very dynamic team leader but also one of the best "people persons" I have met. His great strength was his totally genuine desire to help staff progress in their careers. He would at times make life quite difficult for himself recruitment-wise because of his drive to move people onwards and upwards in their career but I could not help but admire the way he did this, totally unselfishly, since he proved on many occasions that he cared deeply about the development of his staff. Needless to say he gained a great reputation as a manager and ironically some stayed with him precisely for that reason! He helped me to find a position in Gloucester when my only other choice would have been London at the time. As I did not fancy London life after coming from rural Yorkshire, I was delighted to settle in the South West which is where I have been ever since the middle of the 1980s.

Another great leader from my earlier, formative career years that I would wish to mention was Dave Ratcliffe who ran a large, national team of sales engineers within a well-established engineering group. Dave was wonderful at interviewing and showed me how to treat people like few had ever done up to that point. Anyone coming out of any sort of interview with Dave must have felt like they were the most important person in the world! He made people feel completely welcome and treated them in that classic manner of making them feel totally special and unique. Although he was insanely busy, he had an amazing knack of setting aside as much time as was needed to ensure the individual had the very best attention and opportunity to say whatever they felt they needed to say. To me this was sheer professionalism.

I attended the funeral of Larry, a truly charismatic leader for many of my teaching years. Some three thousand others also attended as a huge vote of gratitude and a deep mark of respect. This individual, an undeniably resolute and committed leader, seemed to leave the door open to all and yet still managed to run a large structured organisation through a leadership team of 10 to 12 senior staff. No mean feat that.

Certainly for me a disciplined and tight team in which each person knows their function and role can be highly effective as evidenced, for example, by some of the better football teams. The Barcelona football teams of recent times have seemed to produce a good fusion of the individual prima donna with the hardworking team member. In fairness, they were also managed by some highly talented leaders who had in some cases worn the shirt themselves and so knew fully what the motto "More than a club" really signified.

Sir Alex Ferguson had considerable success in winning trophies at Manchester United, although I remember he had a fairly rocky start after leaving Aberdeen. Not everyone liked his style any more than they might have liked the style of other noteworthy football legends such as Brian Clough at Nottingham Forest and Derby or Bill Shankly at Liverpool but all of them must surely have gained the players' respect in whichever way they engineered it.

You could also add that a strongly rule-based and disciplined approach, which was evident in the cases I have mentioned, paid dividends, particularly in that era. In a modern era of superstar millionaire players who in some cases do not really need to play to be able to afford their bills, particularly in many of the wealthier Premier League clubs, some might propose a less autocratic style of leadership...perhaps based more on motivation and encouragement than fear or trepidation. Having said that, others still would point to several successful modern managers who even today still run the "tight ship" model of management.

I think talented individuals need to feel an absence of any sort of straight jacket, need to be kept fully informed of all new developments and must be allowed to feel that they have been fully consulted prior to a decision being taken rather than seemingly consulted when in fact a decision has already been made some time back. Even among some inner sanctums there may be those who are left out or kept ill-informed for obvious reasons of power and control.

Is a great individual better or more important than a good team? In a Harvard Business Review blog from 2011, Jeff Stiebel, then CEO of Dunn and Bradstreet, responded to several arguments about the value of individuals and teams. In particular he commented on Bill Taylor's view that great people are overrated which was in response to Facebook CEO Mark Zuckerberg's contention at that time that one great engineer is worth one thousand average engineers.

Stiebel made some salient points about quality being more important than quantity when it comes to people. He argued that our brains work well individually but can tend to break down in groups, and individuals follow an inverse rule relative to networks of people. According to Metcalfe's Law the value of a network is proportional to the square of the number of people in the network. According to Reed's Law the value of any individual within a network grows exponentially with every new member. With individuals the opposite was true, Stiebel argued, and the value of a contributor decreased with each additional person contributing to a single project, idea or innovation. He concluded that leaders needed to make tough decisions all the time and so the key was to find the best people and empower them to do great things.

Although I am unlikely to witness the management of a major bridge in its construction phase, I would love to be a fly on the wall (or perhaps a fly on a girder) in order to listen to the best managers getting the best out of a team.

I was, however, privileged to witness, during in the summer of 2013, the outcome of a remarkable bridge restoration project in Somerset. The bridge in question is Tarr Steps, one of a fascinating genre of clapper bridges. Clapper bridges, probably derived from Anglo-Saxon words for heaps of stones, are mainly specific to the United Kingdom. They were often built in rural areas to ford streams or rivers. In the case of bridges such as Tarr Steps they were designed as a walkway usually of flat granite stones weighing up to several tonnes and supported on pillars of stone with slanted cutwaters to break the force of the stream or river in its wilder modes.

The reconstruction of Tarr Steps is quite remarkable as it extended up to fifty-five meters across the river Barle and the seventeen walkway blocks range from one to two tonnes each. Dating this bridge is difficult. Some push for it being medieval, others think the Bronze age or earlier. Legend has it that Old Nick (the Devil) himself had built it and threatened to kill anyone trying to cross it. The local parson was called for. A cat was sent over but apparently vaporised while trying to cross. The parson eventually met the Devil half way and although the Devil uttered profanities at him he gave as good as he got. In the end the Devil allowed the bridge to be crossed unless he himself wished to sunbathe!

The bridge had been damaged on several occasions by trees swept down the river during stormy periods. It was repaired in 1952 by a team of 50 army personnel following damage sustained in the 1940s. In 1952 the team of 50 took some two months to repair it. I was fortunate to speak with the principal contractor of Crestmoor Construction who, along with Somerset County Council's Bridge Engineer and a team of only 7 engineers, repaired and restored it in February 2013 after some of the worst winter storms in 60 years. How long did the repairs take? Only 6 days! Modern technology (including a 13 ton excavator which might have helped considerably back in 1952) together with a team of skilled engineers ensured not only a fast repair but an incredibly cost-effective one too. At around only £10,000 this repair work was superb value given that a new footbridge would very likely have cost in the order of £500,000! I was told how the team had a real eco-logical challenge, for example in their use of bio-degradable oils in their construction equipment, as they needed to be aware of trout and salmon in the river.

From my many and various employments covering Public and Private sectors, Head Offices and Field teams, I personally always loved the warm feeling of being told that as professionals you knew your job and here was yet another opportunity that day to go out and show it. Good team man-agers do this often!

In Year 13 my A-Level students in their final year at school study Busi-ness Ethics. Many of them have part-time jobs and one of the things we often discuss is the approach of some of their ethically "good" employers. Names of some leading retail organisations come up frequently and it is pleasing to hear that they, like many other organisations, believe in get-ting their managers to listen carefully to staff suggestions, either in a team "huddle" or briefing setting, often rewarding staff who offer ideas which can be implemented to improve the smooth running of the organisation. Highly motivational I suggest.

The physical bridges I have described, as a small representation of the world's bridge population, seem to have enjoyed a good deal of success in doing what they were designed to, that is connecting communities, reducing distance between groups of people or uniting one community with another more easily over the course of history.

Jean-Pierre Vernant, the French historian, argues that bridges also have symbolic value:

"To cross a bridge, a river or a border is to leave behind the familiar, personal and comfortable and enter the unknown, a different and strange world where, faced with another reality, we may well find ourselves bereft of home and identity."

—Jean-Pierre Vernant

Wordsworth's famous poem *Composed upon Westminster Bridge* reflects to a large extent the move from country to city life. The changes implicit in that move involved the creation of a complete new social identity often within a radically different cultural setting.

Therefore aside from the purely physical structures we have come to know, I think bridges symbolize life and death, part of a journey or its end, a link with a heaven or a "better place". The crossing of a bridge has often been regarded as in some way a test of character or worthiness. Thinking back to the classic "Lemmings" computer game where the aim was to get them into Lemming heaven, a place of ultimate safety, the concept of paradise may reflect the end of the final stage for the human journey. A few Lemmings sadly used to fall by the wayside ending up in fiery furnaces, dark chasms or the bottomless pits of the game. The exponents of that game ensured maximum numbers reached their final destination safely.

The Judgement Bridge known as Chinvat in Zoroastrianism assesses human nature at its deepest level. The words and life actions from each person's soul are known to Mithra, Saroosh and Rashnu, the three angels that guard each person's core values. Rashnu's scales of justice decide the width of each person's bridge. The good are often escorted to heaven by a beautiful young woman. The bad cross their ever narrowing bridge until they fall into hell.

In Islam, the Bridge of Jahannam is a bridge to paradise said to be "narrower than a spider's thread and sharper than a sword". The wicked are said to fall to hell while the good make safe passage into heaven.

In Norse legend, Heimdallr guards the rainbow bridge known as Bifrost which connects Midgard to Asgard. The bridge has an element of fire designed to keep out those who are not worthy of safe arrival in Asgard.

Sometimes the crossing of the bridge is part of a descent to an underworld or watery place in the form of a rescue act. In Hinduism, Hanuman, the monkey king in the Ramayana, builds a bridge for Rama to rescue his queen Sita.

"O'er the deep sea where monsters play, a bridge O Rama will I lay"

The dangerous and monstrous Ravana was defeated by Rama thanks largely to the sacrificial act of Hanuman.

In the Knight of the Cart by Chrétien de Troyes, Sir Lancelot and Sir Gawain, two of the greatest knights in the legends of King Arthur, are on a quest to rescue Queen Guinevere who has been captured by Meleagant, a powerful enemy knight, and taken to Gorre, a place which can only be accessed when great trials and suffering have been undergone. Two dangerous bridges lead to the place: 'the Underwater Bridge', a narrow bridge that is half the depth of the river that isolates Gorre from land, and the terrifying 'Sword Bridge' in the form of a sharp sword. The 'Knight of the Cart' (Lancelot in disguise) gives Gawain the choice of bridge, and he chooses the 'Underwater Bridge' which is marginally the easier of the two, leaving the Sword Bridge for Lancelot.

Using the symbolic vehicle of bridges, the levels of courage, leadership and valour typified by the sacrifice of these knights, together with the unselfish actions of those such as the monkey king Hanuman, combine to show a chivalrous and wonderful side of human nature.

The Stanzas of Dzyan are an ancient text supposedly of Tibetan origin. Some argue they are of a darker side and so are to be taken warily. However my contention that the above-mentioned bridges are links between gods and men, those who strive or judge, rescuers and the rescued are perhaps summed up in the idea of Svabhavat in which oneness is achieved by the crossing of these bridges.

"It is within the realm of refined human consciousness that the full bridge, from above and below, can be realized, crossed and extended even when the two have become the One".

Such bridges as these all have some commonality of symbolic theme about the journey itself and the bliss of journey's end, together with several cautionary motifs about what happens to those who live life in the wrong way.

When we taught the Conflict and Reconciliation module, the references to bridges were virtually all positive ones. Reconciliation could be studied from a religious angle or not. It was perhaps well symbolised by the concept of bridge building especially between individuals or communities that had fallen out with each other or damaged each other in the past and now had some sort of chance to put things right or restore what was lost.

In a religious context, this patching up of relationships was also of course applied to the need for the Judaeo-Christian community to patch up its relationship with the Creator which at times through sin had become damaged. In that tradition, the idea of the God of the Old Testament offering a protective berith or Covenant was important. God would protect and guide the people in return for obedience to God's Laws, symbolised in the Ten Commandments, and faithful allegiance. Not easy! Indeed the Bible is full of incidents highlighting the way God's people allowed themselves to be seduced by "other gods" and the way that there was always a bridge back to the one true God when people came to their senses and were forgiven, for example the story of the Prodigal Son in Luke's Gospel or the story of Adulterous woman in John's Gospel. In truth this is still continuing today as true followers not only of Christianity but of the other many world religions make their efforts to get their lives on track in the pursuit of what they believe to be ultimately important, while those of no little or faith try equally hard in very many cases to act in a tolerant and loving manner towards others as the excellent humanists they are trying to be.

When Simon and Garfunkel released the album "Bridge over Troubled Water" in the 1970s, the title song was noteworthy for being at No 1 simultaneously in the USA and UK. It was 6 weeks at No 1 in the USA and 3 weeks in the UK.

This song is one of the most covered songs in history. All the greats have done it. Yet it was quite a simple set of lyrics especially in the opening lines, which propelled it towards its legendary status.

"When you're weary, feeling small, when tears are in your eyes I will dry them all"

The song talks of having our tears dried in the tough situations in which life places us where we become worn and tired and our self-esteem is reduced. I often used to get my students to draw their bridge and show their troubled waters beneath. They would invariably produce some powerful examples from their own lives and the lives of those around them. Typically for teenagers issues of relationships, alcohol, smoking and drugs could appear among those troubled waters. Their fragility and humanity appeared with honesty and trust and hopefully mine did too.

It was very similar when they used clay kinaesthetically (actually making something physical) to represent themselves as a broken pot, a reference to Jeremiah at the potter's house in the Old Testament. Here the idea was that just as the potter could rebuild, remould, reshape the damaged clay on the wheel, so God could shape the lives of those who believed and trusted in the skills of their Creator to help them get their lives back on track. Some of the pots they created were amazing and showed their beauty and uniqueness and at the same time the flaws and damage caused them by the troubled waters of life. This could be quite touching at times and really quite humbling. Excellent teachers do not have all the answers and education is far from mere instruction.

According to where they were on their spiritual journey, the bridge could represent their family or those whom they trusted to get them through the tough parts and for some their faith in Jesus. The well-known "Footprints" prayer suggested that during the times of heaviest trial when only one set of footprints appeared on the beach and it seemed that God had abandoned us, there was actually only one set of footprints because God was carrying us through the trials and tribulations of life.

As a teacher, I used to feel incredibly privileged to be part of their lives in guiding such tasks but also mindful that it was about listening to them and where they were before any attempt was made to present a Christian perspective for discussion and reflection. My duty was always, I believed, to do things this way round. Margaret Donaldson was the pedagogy guru for me. Her idea of going in through their door and bringing them out through your own always sat well with me, but I stress the key to this approach was listening carefully to where students were in their life journey, fully respecting them in that and then presenting ideas for challenge and debate but never with the intention to force or indoctrinate. If students felt they could express their views freely and honestly but with respect from all students in the class then the learning could at times be extremely powerful.

Many years ago, one student aged 14 trusted me enough to write me a poem describing her feelings at losing her mother. I still have it to this day. It was a heartfelt poem in which she talked about all the ways her mother helped the family, made sacrifices and taught them everything she knew except how to cope after she died. To me this showed a remarkable and heartfelt honesty from one so young.

However, one point I also wish to emphasise here is that even though we generally took a positive line on the role of bridge building in the Christian tradition as a tool to reconciliation or forgiveness, some bridges exist which were actually built without any concept of reconciliation in mind at all. I refer, for example, to the Kapelbrücke or Chapel Bridge in Lucerne, Switzerland as it would be called in English.

At the time of writing I have not visited this bridge but I gather that, built in the early 1300s, it was originally a 285 metre covered wooden trestle bridge on wooden piles and stone piers to provide and complete a line of defence for the city over the river Reuss. The city walls ran North and South of the river, hence the need for a defensive bridge to form part of the walls. It is Europe's oldest wooden trestle bridge, and so it was greatly to my surprise when I read that much of it was destroyed by fire as late as 1993, possibly from a cigarette. Happily it was restored and the famous water tower in the centre was largely preserved.

That started me thinking what "burning bridges" means. I am sure there have been many other bridges in the course of history which have been burned down either accidently or more likely deliberately (arson), and that was one bridge which was burnt down but thankfully rebuilt.

"Burning bridges" is often taken as a metaphor to represent the making of choices or decisions which cannot be changed in the future, or acting in such a way that in leaving, your return will never be welcomed.

"If we burn our bridges prematurely we will have crossed to the other side only in a delusive sense while our consciousness remains ever behind. There is no rung in the ladder of knowledge that can be skipped"

(Theosophy Trust)

In warfare, bridges were of course often booby-trapped or mined so that they would blow up when the enemy tried to pursue which would become impossible if the bridge blew. In the race to Berlin at the end of World War 2, the bridge at Remagen, one the Germans did everything they could to destroy to hold up the Allied liberators' march towards Berlin, springs to mind. In relationships we may have acted in a similar fashion, rendering it impossible for the relationship to be repaired depending on our intention on leaving it once we were across. Maybe we decided to set it on fire by what we said or some "final straw" act which ensured nobody could follow us. Some are glad, some are sad at this final act. Music puts it like this….

Status Quo:

"Burning bridges never made me cry, I could walk away with no goodbye"

The Foo Fighters:

"These are my famous last words! My number's up, bridges all burned"

Drama puts it well too. Tom Stoppard's existentialist tragicomedy "Rosencrantz and Guildenstern Are Dead", which had its premiere as part of the Edinburgh Fringe Festival in 1966, majors on two courtiers who represent characters from Shakespeare's Hamlet. The two characters spend the entire play quite confused as to their own identities. Themes in Stoppard's play include free will and determinism (the idea that our lives are controlled rather than free, with the causal chain of events dictating all our behaviours and ethics), the difficulty of making meaningful choices in life, art and reality, insignificance and the seemingly meaningless nature of existence. Guildenstern appears to suggest that our obstacles in life become distant memories quickly as we build them up to be huge but they disappear as quickly as they arise:

"We cross our bridges when we come to them and burn them behind us, with nothing to show for our progress except a memory of the smell of smoke, and a presumption that once our eyes watered"

Aside, then, from the purely physical constructions, vital though they are, it seems clear to me (and infinitely preferable to burning them) that we are far better people when we spend more of our time trying to build bridges symbolically in our minds to connect better with others i.e. perhaps improving our relationships with other individuals or groups. Indeed we can shorten the distance between our differences in a symbolic way without even lifting a stone, a wooden plank or a piece of sheet steel or aluminium. For some, as we have seen, connecting with paradise or heaven (if we believe in the concept) is also a motivator for building our bridges with others as it may determine whether paradise is indeed our ultimate destination or not.

Chapter 2   The Alienation Effect

"Never build a wall until you are sure what you are walling in and what you are walling out"

Robert Frost

Walls like bridges come in many shapes, sizes and materials. The functions of such walls have been very varied, ranging from providing a definition of an area and protecting its inhabitants, to providing some kind of control by keeping some in and keeping others out. Whilst most are fixed, some are portable. There are retaining walls, shared walls, boundary walls, border walls, cavity walls and fire walls just to name but a few.

I taught at a German Grammar School near Hannover in northern Germany during the academic year 1973/4. It was a real character-forming year for me as I had never lived abroad before. The school was in the region known as the Lüneburg Heath. It was a popular tourist destination especially when the heathland was in full bloom. This lovely forested and heathland area bordered onto the Zonengrenze, the fence separating East and West Germany which was built in 1961. (In Berlin there was also major separation between Eastern and Western zones of the City with an actual wall through some areas which led to some very creative attempts by would-be escapees.)

I must admit it felt very strange to me in the autumn of 1973 only to be able to travel in one of three directions and never eastwards. This was certainly a new one on me, very odd. The road leading east suddenly petered out before you saw the fence staring right at you. The border fence had been constructed with towers, minefields and dogs along many of its stretches. Some of it dissected villages and consequently had split communities and it would be many years until the Berlin Wall came down (which one of my Professors at University was adamant would never happen) and the fences with it and at least some people could be re-united with their families.

I was involved heavily during the school year as a Teaching Assistant and was only in my early twenties therefore, somewhat unfortunately, I did not find the opportunity to visit Berlin. This would certainly have proved difficult at that time due to the need for visas and a strictly monitored itinerary with East German border guards present at each of the limited border crossing points.

As one of my main leisure interests, when I was not teaching, I used to read widely and my interest had always been drawn to European literature. Included in this genre were the contemporary modern German and Swiss playwrights Bertolt Brecht, Max Frisch and Friedrich Dürrenmatt. These three modern dramatists wrote plays which sparked my imagination with overtones of the absurd, banal, strange and scary.

I watched a performance in German of Bertolt Brecht's Dreigroschenoper (Threepenny Opera) in which most of the action took place in a cage suspended above the stage. Very strange and off beat! In Die Physiker, three brilliant physicists consider that they have become too unstable and damaged to be allowed out into the public and therefore vow to stay voluntarily in their asylum.

Publikumsbeschimfung (roughly translated as Offending the Audience) was a German play which like many of its kind broke the mould of classical theatre by close interaction of the actors with the audience but in that particular play the emphasis was on ensuring the audience did not become emotionally involved in the play. Indeed, with no real script and actors who were often unrecognisable from members of the audience, it was new and different at the time and made many feel quite uncomfortable, which was precisely its aim. The Theatre of the Absurd, as it was known, became famous for its ability to alienate. It was known by many as Verfremdungseffekt (Alienation effect) particularly within the Epic Theatre of Brecht.

I also enjoyed reading some of the works of Franz Kafka. This complex author from the former Czechoslovakia in the early 1900s wrote some interesting and often rather strange works, in many cases dealing with the topic of the perceived alienation and isolation of the individual in society at different levels.

In Die Verwandlung (The Transformation), Gregor Samsa is a boy who upon waking one morning realises he has been transformed into a beetle. The story reflects at first a sense of shock which becomes upset and then anger as his family gradually turn against him. At one stage an apple is thrown at him by a member of his family which sticks in his back and rots away. He becomes isolated in every way: - physically, emotionally, spiritually as his family struggle to come to terms with such a major disruption to their comfortable routines.

In Das Schloss (The Castle) the theme of alienation is again evident as the main protagonist known only as K (Kafka himself perhaps?) attempts to gain access to the authorities in a fairly remote castle near a village which the authorities appear to control for reasons which are never fully explained to the reader. For many the castle walls represents man's mainly futile attempts to wrestle with some seemingly omnipotent bureaucratic systems in the attempted pursuit of an (in any case) unobtainable aim.

The story abounds with crossed wires and misunderstandings, village taboos, secrecies and paperwork inaccuracies. K, whom the reader is led to believe is a land surveyor, is victim to all of this and especially to the character known as Klamm (whose name in Czech and German suggests illusion, locks, secrecy or barriers). Most of the story is about K's fruitless attempts to secure a meeting with Klamm, his castle contact, which only frustrate and dismay him. For some, K's efforts to enter the castle walls suggest a theological theme of salvation. For others, the story is more about the need for friendship and the pain of solitude and rejection. Some of the villagers might appear to be helpful in his quest but in reality are not and his plans are constantly thwarted.

In the late 1960s a cult TV show in England called The Prisoner saw an ex-spy brilliantly played by Patrick McGoohan resign very suddenly from a secret intelligence agency in London only to be kidnapped and held in a distant "village" from which escape was continually discouraged. Other spies were similarly held against their will there. Number 6, as he was known to ensure anonymity in the village, was always seen to be questioning authority, rebelling and trying to discover the identity of number 1. A succession of Number 2s steadfastly refused to reveal Number 1's identity. There seemed for me to be some overlaps between Kafka's castle and the village of the Prisoner, although unlike K in the Castle, Number 6 in The Prisoner did escape in the end.

Back in 1973 literature and music also reflected, very cleverly in many cases, the themes of alienation and isolation in society. At the Grammar School where I was teaching there were very few resources available to me to use in class and most of what I used I had brought myself from home. Among the most useful of these was the newly released album by Pink Floyd "The Dark side of the Moon", later to be followed by "The Wall".

Several tracks appealed to the students especially at Sixth Form level not only because English progressive rock was cult in West Germany at the time (I do not know about East Germany but suspect it was harder to get hold of) but also because of the wide-ranging philosophical themes and excellent lyrics. Germany has of course provided many of the world's great philosophers and ethicists. The dark side was not intended to refer to the physical side of the moon which is in shadow as much as the shadowy side of our human selves represented by the untimely decline in the health and well-being of former band member Syd Barrett who died in 2006 with drug use and mental illness postulated as reasons contributing to his early death.

Greed and consumerism are mocked in "Money", "Us and Them" looks at the symbolism of conflict and the isolation of the depressed, "Breathe" talks of solitude and withdrawal, "Time" warns those who focus on the mundane that the years slip by all too quickly and the a decades are gone before we know it, while "Eclipse" at the end focuses on thinking of others as one of the possible and better common traits of humanity.

Leading on from that, The Wall was a concept album from 1979 which was also made into a film. Pink is a rock opera character, in part modelled on bass player Roger Waters, suffering from an overprotective mother, abusive teachers and marriage breakdown all contributing to a self-imposed isolation from society represented by different bricks in a wall. It is claimed that this wall was a symbol of an earlier tour in 1977 when Waters became frustrated with an over exuberant audience close to the stage and wished he could construct a wall between himself as performer and the audience.

In any "famous walls" quiz, the Great Wall (or more properly Walls) of China will certainly be on everyone's answer sheet, and thereafter the Western or Wailing Wall in Jerusalem, the Berlin Wall and probably Hadrian's Wall (if you are completing the quiz in the UK). Other top walls of the world include the walls of Troy in Turkey, Babylon in modern Iraq and Sacsayhuaman in Peru.

So then why was Humpty Dumpty sitting on one? In the nursery rhyme he falls off the wall and cannot be put back together, not even by all the Kings horses and all the Kings men. Was this just a simple rhyme to amuse children? Perhaps there was more to it than that. There are several suggestions as to the real meaning. As always conjecture and debate are healthy and it is wise to approach such explanations with an open mind.

From the historical point of view, one suggestion is that Humpty Dumpty was in fact a "tortoise" style siege engine used in an unsuccessful attempt to besiege the walls of Parliament held in Gloucester. Another version is that Humpty Dumpty was a cannon place on the walls of Colchester in the siege of the town in 1648 and that it fell off the wall when the wall was hit by a Parliamentary cannon which all the Royalist and Cavalier defenders could not put it back as it was too heavy.

In other explanations of the meaning, the anthropomorphic egg (egg in human form) is not used to describe Humpty Dumpty as it was possibly a riddle of the time. The egg could however be taken as a symbol of fertility and potential and the fall could represent man's fall from grace with the need for a saviour to restore it from its brokenness to wholeness again. It might be argued that only God could allow the egg to fulfil its full and true potential.

Many stories are cleverly written so as to be able to be read by children of all ages. The Selfish Giant by Oscar Wilde is a story which has been used to encourage young and old alike to think about their attitude to posses-sions and their acceptance, tolerance and love of others. We used to use it with our year 7 students aged 11 to 12 on reflective retreat days off-site. The giant is away visiting an ogre friend in Cornwall and in his seven year absence some children come and play in his garden bringing their youthful joy and life into it. On his return he comes to hate the children's presence and builds a wall to keep them out. As a result of his actions, the garden symbolically falls into winter, only broken when the children find a gap in the wall. The children are afraid of the giant though and run away, apart from one who tries to climb a tree. The giant helps him, sees the errors of his ways and knocks down the wall. Spring returns but the boy does not and the giant is heartbroken.

One day the giant sees a tree with white blossom in the garden with the boy lying beneath it and bearing the stigmata (wounds of Jesus). The boy tells him that because he let him come and play in his garden the giant would be welcomed into his garden (Paradise) and this happens after a happy giant dies and is found himself under the same tree covered in white blossoms.

The Selfish Giant has been interpreted as echoing some of the issues in Oscar Wilde's own life, especially his awareness of the beauty of the world and its people juxtaposed with Wilde's apparent inability to live the virtuous life such beauty requires. The giant (like children of all ages) needs to understand that love cannot be about the selfish retention of possessions but can surely only blossom fully when it is given away and shared with others. This is evidenced by the stigmata which for many Christians represent the love Christ showed for everyone by his vicarious suffering and death on the Cross (a freely-willed atonement for the sins of others to make humanity whole or right again). It is interesting to read about people who have discovered real happiness at the times in their lives when they have become aware of the needs of others and have found the will to help them. As examples of this I can point to many celebrities who have been deeply touched by their own journeys to poorer parts of Africa to take part in projects in support of Comic Relief and other such excellent ventures.

Clearly the building of physical walls or fences has in often kept communities divided and therefore arguably weakened or subdued. There exists much alienation today in Britain even though many still regard it as a land of opportunity and equality. As I write this, one political party would sooner abolish the Human Rights Act and replace it with a British Rights Bill so that Britain could make its own local decisions in these areas rather than be controlled from Strasbourg as part of the European Union. That obviously brings with it a string of problems but not wishing at this point to become too political I shall instead focus on some types of alienation which affect many if not all of us at times.

We don't need to look very far to find examples of physical and symbolical walls causing alienation and isolation. People who live alone in tower block apartments with some of them some hardly knowing their neighbours. What about people with genuine disabilities who have been informed that the rules have changed and their claims are no longer valid? Those who have in good faith applied for one rate of interest only to find out that that they have received a different rate because their application was through no fault of their own delayed in the post? Then again what about those company telephone lines with three options to choose from, then a further five options then four then at long last possibly the one required-or maybe not? On several occasions I have experienced that irritating sense of frustration and being kept at bay which is felt by so many of us raging against the apparent might of the administration machine which seems to keeps us right where it wants to, although they might argue they were unable to run things differently due to their volumes of calls, numbers of patients, incidences of customers waiting to book or to cancel and so on.

When thousands of song contest tickets, rare Wimbledon debentures or much prized World Cup tickets can be sold out literally in minutes, where does that leave those unlucky ones who were as desperate as anyone else to see their hero or heroes? Even more so those who thought they had provided the correct details on the on-line form only to be informed (or worse left to guess) that they had been unsuccessful because details were incorrect, passwords invalid, or dates apparently ticked wrongly.

I claim to be no expert on financial or banking systems. Much has been made of the economic downturn which has affected the world since 2008/9 and continues to do so. As I write this, I am no wiser than many other of my generation about state pension forecasts, the likelihood of decent savings rates or the changing ways in which pension pots are to be freed up to use as if they were bank accounts, a far cry from annuities markets which have undergone such radical reform. Therefore I am not particularly interested in singling out any one party which might or might not be responsible for the downturn. So why include ideas about the financial world at all then? Just as K in Das Schloss seems to realise he is faced with a seemingly controlling and dominating bureaucracy, so many have similarly found it hard to come to terms with what has happened to their money and who has had possession of it since the downturn.

Fannie Mae and Freddie Mac, two huge National Federal Mortgage Associations in the USA, were financial organisations placed into Government sponsored enterprises in 2008 following a crisis in the subprime mortgage market and the subsequent shock collapse of giant investment bank Lehman Brothers. The value of preferred shares owned by many commercial banks in Fannie and Freddie collapsed, global stock markets were hit hard and the effects are still being felt today around the planet. The consequences have been massive. In the UK at least part of our current national debt running somewhere between £1.4 and £1.5 trillion or 80% or more of GDP, more than doubling in the last 20 years, arguably has its origins in the lack of fiscal prudence shown by some of the global financial sectors and their leaders. At one stage in the UK it was possible to borrow seven times salary for a mortgage! It doesn't take the genius of Einstein to work out the likely dangers of that level of debt.

In 2013 the UK's credit rating was downgraded and the current Government have indicated they think it will be at least 2017 or 2018 before the structural debt is eliminated. The outlook is not promising. Indeed, it could be argued that most of us are living beyond our means. Payments on plastic over the Internet have exploded as more of us than ever buy products or services on long term deals. There was originally a system where a small deposit-style part (or none) of the cost was paid straight away with the remainder paid off in very small and regular amounts until nothing remained to be paid. The advantage was obviously that you were enjoying using the product or service rather than having to save up and wait for it and had almost forgotten about payment by the time the debt was cleared especially as it was in small and supposedly affordable chunks.

However, many of us have simultaneously used a lot more of these payment arrangements than is good for us, our eyes being bigger than our wallets, you might say. To some today my comments may sound anachronistic. This is probably because I was brought up believing you should buy what you can afford and when you saved up and waited you actually heightened the joy of eventually making the purchase. Those who would disagree with me would argue that there is nothing wrong with the instant gratification concept "I want it all and I want it now". I am not playing "Holier than Thou" here either, though, because I too succumb on some occasions to online shopping though I am fairly disciplined and budget carefully each month to try and ensure I am not living beyond my means!

The development of social media, which is in part about interaction and networking among people sharing their lives through information and comment, has fuelled massive increases in usage of the Internet and mobile phones. There have been some interesting social media alternatives to Dale Carnegie's famous 1936 book title "How to win friends and influence people". These include, for example, the 2008 film title "How to lose friends and alienate people" and the cleverly named "How to win Likes and alienate people" an article by Steve Ranger from 2012 in which he questions the value (to business in particular) of a "Like" on Facebook. As the number of Likes now exceeds 2 billion per day, it seems appropriate to question what a "Like " is actually worth and whether it is of any use procuring fake "Likes" to enable a business to appear more successful, attractive or whatever a "Like" is supposed to signify (which seems far from clear cut anyway).

Nomophobia is a term coined to define the fear someone may have of literally having no mobile and being therefore unable to access the Internet or communicate with whomever they might wish to be in touch with at the time. It can leave some people with a sense of fear or panic as genuine as any other phobia. I can imagine a modern version of K in Kafka's Das Schloss outside the castle walls realising he has lost his mobile. Desolation! One has to ask whether it is worth our while to be able to connect so often and so easily when a lack of connection through a loss of signal, misplacing of phone or internet problems can leave people feeling genuinely lost and just as alone as if they were on their own desert island.

One of the biggest challenges within social media for all of us is to rationalise and make sense of the increasingly blurred lines between what can be termed the experiencing and what can be termed the documenting of our lives and our obsession with the latter to the detriment of the former. Some might argue that the constant documenting of our activities and thoughts, especially the more mundane ones, are making us more narcissistic or self-obsessed. Excessively tweeting or blogging is arguably both an addiction and a waste of time which we could be using for more and better quality lived experiences while dumbing down our intellect until we need to comment on some quite banal, everyday fact. Some would go further and argue that the more we communicate in ways that obviate the need for face to face contact, the less human we become and the more isolated from each other (dumping your partner or sacking employees by text for example).

Whilst there are many brilliant aspects of mobile communication, one of the saddest examples of the whole social media debate that I have come across features the actress Yvette Vickers. I read about her in an article by Stephen Marche entitled "Is Facebook making us lonely?" (April 2012) A former Playboy pin-up star, this B-list actress starred as a femme fatale in two late 1950s cult horror films "Attack of the 50 foot Woman" and "Attack of the Giant Leeches". She was found dead in her home in Los Angeles circa 2010 aged nearly 83. She had not been seen for a long time and was discovered by a neighbour who had noticed old letters in her letter box starting to turn yellow. The mummified state of her body indicated she might have been dead for close to a year. A space heater was still left on as was her computer.

Within two weeks her death was the subject of over 16,000 Facebook posts and nearly 900 tweets. Having withdrawn from her extended family, this private person had sadly received more attention in death than in the final years of her life, having made calls not to friends and family but to distant fans who had found her through fan conventions and Internet sites. Ironically it seems the more connected we have become the lonelier it is possible to be. Within her own four walls too. How sad.

Following the Pink Floyd theme, the concept of a wall might seem quite an appropriate obstacle in many of these above situations. However, my sense of frustration at the lack of being able to travel eastwards in Germany must have paled into total insignificance when compared to the alienated feelings of those on the wrong side of two of the best-known walls in the world, namely Hadrian's Wall and the Great Wall(s) of China, possibly the most famous of them all.

The Roman Empire was one of the biggest and most powerful the world has known. The Hadrian's Wall Country website refers to "the most magnificent and best preserved of Rome's great frontiers" and an "*epic story of an Empire boasting Imperial ambition, personal dreams, political intrigue and commercial exploitation on a scale not seen until modern times.*" I was fortunate to visit Hadrian's Wall on a lovely hot summer day a few years ago. The fort at Housesteads is at a fairly central point in the remains of the wall, although originally I understand there was a fort in the wall about every four miles. While it was a glorious place to be on a fine summer day, I have often thought it must have been one of the least popular postings of the Roman Army in the middle of winter, compared with a tour of duty in, for example, sunny southern France or Italy. Granted those areas can be cold and wet at times too, and I did experience snow in Montpellier as early as half term during one autumn holiday. Nevertheless, Roman soldiers, more at home with milder Mediterranean climates, might well have found it tough going in our "frozen north".

Hadrian's Wall was started in AD 122 during the reign of the emperor of that name. Hadrian's biographer wrote that it was built to separate the Romans from the barbarians. There is much speculation over whether a wall 80 miles long was actually the best way to deal with the northern tribes of Picks and Scots. The layout and positioning of the wall in certain places suggests it was not always necessarily built solely for defence. In any case, building and guarding such a construction would have had significant economic implications.

Raids were arguably not a hugely worrying threat from a relatively thinly populated border region, with whom some treaties were agreed in any event, so it may have had more to do with the Roman army laying down markers to delineate the boundaries of the Empire, possibly more necessary in areas like Egypt and Palestine where there had been rebellious uprisings. A boundary around the Empire would naturally assist with the control and monitoring of smuggling and illegal immigration. Possibly in similar fashion to Roman walls constructed in other locations of image significance, Hadrian's Wall sent out a clear message that Roman was the superpower of its day and was not to be trifled with.

Some say you can see the 13,000 miles of the Great Wall of China from the moon, others disagree and suggest that it can barely been seen from the edges of earth's atmosphere. What there might be less disagreement about however is the fact this set of walls, probably started in the 7th century BC, together forms the longest man made structure/ defensive fortification on earth, allegedly also being the costliest in terms of the million or more who died in the construction process. The prime purpose would seem to have been to defend the Chinese Empire from Manchu and Mongolian incursions from the north.

The Wall was never included in the seven wonders of the ancient world but is usually featured in lists of wonders of the medieval world. However, the list of those involved in building it is interesting and includes guards, peasants, disgraced noblemen, prisoners and the unemployed. During the latter of the three dynasties Qin, Han and Ming, it is reputed to have been defended by around a million Empire soldiers against barbarians and non-Chinese tribes. It is as high as 30 feet in places and varies in width from around 15 to 30 feet. The Wall rises from sea level in places to over 500 metres. Several temples were built along it dedicated to Guandi the war god. Badaling is often quoted as the most visited section. Pictures of the Wall often feature Jiankou section as it is a steep and winding section and is particularly impressive. Once again some of the key objectives in building these walls may be more allied to delineating frontiers and showing off the power of empires.

"*Stone walls do not a prison make nor iron bars a cage*"

(Richard Lovelace)

This quote seems to suggest that it is our minds that determine how we interpret situations in life. Thinking and believing we can act freely is a basic human instinct, a fact I will return to in Chapter 5. Philosopher John

Locke's example of a sleeping man in a locked room refers. On waking he makes a conscious decision to stay in the room. In reality he could have done no other as he was unaware that the room was in fact already locked and yet he believes himself to have free will in this choice rather than accepting that things are determined for him.

The stone walls of prisons are themselves a fascinating concept. I think of Alcatraz, the famous rock island 1.5 miles off the coast of San Francisco, for example, from which escape was almost impossible up until it became disused in 1963. Thirty six men apparently tried, twenty three were caught, six shot and killed during their escape. Two drowned. The remaining five went missing also presumed drowned. Why build such walled monsters?

The code of Hammurabi written around 1750BC in Babylon allowed the state to develop sophisticated legal codes which were largely based on the "lex talionis", a code allowing for punishment as revenge or retaliation, sometimes administered by victims. Later on prison reformers such as John Howard attempted to ensure some dignity for prison inmates involving aspects such as cleanliness and privacy which had been lacking in many ancient prisons where chained inmates barely existed in rat-infested damp conditions with little or no food. The great social reformer Jeremy Bentham in the late 1700s devised the sort of prison design on which modern prisons are based, with his Panoptikon, which was a central tower so guards could observe all inmates without themselves being seen. Although the modern prison is not built in quite this way, nevertheless control and observation are still crucial. It was a huge change when prisons were actually used for more than simply holding centres for those awaiting trial or execution.

The key question for us in terms of building prisons in the future (often debated with my Year 11 students at the age of 15 to 16) is whether we should be building more of them or less of them. In other words asking whether they in fact are an effective use of taxpayers' hard-earned money or not. Statistics suggest at least half of those released may well re-offend within a year. Why? The old adage that the punishment must fit the crime in order to be effective seems to me to place a very heavy responsibility on judge and jury to get sentencing right. Too light and prisoners may re-offend thinking they have got away with it, too heavy and they will most likely have been seething with resentment during their time inside and become only too keen to reap revenge on society. Some thinkers call prisons "schools of crime" suggesting that the more naïve inmate may learn valuable new skills while at Her Majesty's pleasure but that those skills are often a lot less desirable than society would like.

In The Prison with symbolic walls: Complexity and Structuration in Václav Havel's Power of the Powerless, there is a wonderfully touching story. Havel (himself no stranger to prisons as a dissident before becoming the first democratically elected president of Czechoslovakia in 1989) was told a story by a dissident prisoner in China about another prisoner who gleaned from the shop floor tiny pieces of glittering wire which he kept in a bottle. Years later when this prisoner was freed he took the bottle as the only thing he had to mark the passage of all those years. He was now too old to work but rose every day at the same time as he had in prison and spent each day as if pacing the tiny cell he had inhabited all those years... four paces forward, four paces back. One day he smashed the bottle to see how many pieces of wire he had collected and wept to find the broken shards of glass reveal merely one clump of wire rusted in the shape of the bottle. Think about it. Here we see clearly not only the effect of prison walls but the effect of power, authority and the control and determination of a person's body, mind, spirit and very existence.

There are times when, like you, I feel deeply alienated and upset at many of the atrocities we have faced and continue to face in society. What gives, or has ever given, anyone the right to massacre the survivors of a town or village during or at the end of a war or conflict when it has been surrounded? Why can the innocent not be taken prisoner rather than be ritually slaughtered? Why do we torture human body, mind and spirit rather than seeking to ennoble them? How can we do this to any human being if we are to call ourselves in any way civilised? Why do some of us in the 21st century still allow ourselves to get seduced by mass hysteria or the pressures of dictators or gang mentalities? Have we really learnt so little about what it means to be human?

The alienation effect which I argue has been manifest in so many different examples of physical and symbolic walls over the centuries, continues to be a highly significant hallmark of life during the previous and current centuries with the paradox that the individual who has become in many cases more isolated, fearful and alienated than in previous times has never been more in need of being part of a team be it a friendship group, local community or nation.

In the 1600s, Philosopher Thomas Hobbes in his treatise on the structure of society and legitimate government which he called Leviathan (a lumbering deep-sea monster), described the life of man as *"solitary, poor, nasty, brutish and short",* a description which might well have resonated with many who had experience of either one or both World Wars in the first half of the 20th century. It was also suggested that humans were savages tamed by society as opposed to French philosopher Rousseau who is reputed to have regarded human beings as angels corrupted by society.

The latter is a somewhat more optimistic view. I often explored these concepts with A-Level Ethics groups. Most of the students were more inclined to side with Rousseau than Hobbes which perhaps might be expected at such a young age. At that age I myself might well have agreed with them. Perhaps I might think slightly differently now. I consider myself lucky to have born in the 1950s in a period of relative peace after Two World Wars however, and I intend to show in the next chapter how one specific ideology built more walls of isolation, alienation and suffering than it is scarcely possible to imagine.

Chapter 3   Afraid to love?

"Love takes off masks that we fear we cannot live without and know we cannot live within"

(James A. Baldwin)

Good teachers are taught to recap at the start of a lesson, something we used to call the golden five minutes. Although I am no psychologist, I understand that for effective cognitive learning to take place, connections need to be made involving our synapses. Provided we have understood the material properly in the first place we are then better able to learn and retain material when networks are built up, adding on to and developing what we already know and understand. Therefore by way of a very brief recap of my first two chapters, in the first I talked mainly about physical and symbolic bridge building and bridge burning, whilst in the chapter you have just read I focussed on the real and symbolic walls which I claim have led at various times to our protection as well as to our isolation and alienation.

Back at the start of the Year 9 syllabus on Conflict and Reconciliation, the lessons during the early part of September would centre on conflict, namely what it is, where it is to be found and what causes it. This made sense since students could hardly begin to understand the challenging concept of the need for reconciliation, especially the Sacrament of Reconciliation in Catholic communities, without first understanding the basic cognitive facts and emotional factors underpinning the nature of conflict in society today. I believe that for students fully to understand issues of Religious Education, experiential learning is just as important as empirical/factual knowledge if you wish them to achieve any depth of empathy with the material. Therefore I would try to use example clips of issues such as road rage, football crowds and bullying in order to investigate and question how and why humans can sometimes behave as animals. I would invite the students to identify the character traits of a range of animals from lions and tigers to chameleons and teddy bears and role play some of them. It was always interesting to watch 14 year olds role-playing teddy who really just wanted to be loved!!

When I was little I used to love cutting out animal masks from cereal packets and threading string through before wearing the mask and feeling what it would be like to be that animal. In the classroom we took the idea of masks to what I believed was an enjoyable and interactive level as we firstly learnt about the many different types of physical mask worn by such as bank robbers, tribal chiefs and superheroes before proceeding to thinking about emotional masks and how we make and wear them ourselves as well as why this might be a problem.

Some students used to put in hours at home on the design and manufacture of their own masks. Many of them of course had experience to draw on from cross-curricular topics such as Art, Drama and English and many had done work on masks at Primary school. Masks to represent football team identities, Scandinavian gods, the weather, their moods and emotions were often brilliantly constructed out of all sorts of resources and painted or decorated. The students' work proudly out on display ("Oh look, there's my mask!") was often noticed and commented on at open evenings by parents who "wished Religious Education had been so interesting in their day".

It went a lot deeper than just display work of course. Students were challenged hard in Religious Education lessons to think about the wearing of masks and just what it might signify. To explain my own thoughts on this I refer to William Golding's "Lord of the Flies" (the name being a direct translation of Beelzebub and another "devil" allusion) a book which proved quite scary when I studied it at school.

A group of schoolboys stranded on a desert island in wartime try to establish and run a society on it with horrendous results. This type of story is often referred to as dystopian where human choices are shown leading to one of two possible futures, good or bad. The choices in this story centre on those between individual well- being and the common good.

In the book, what starts out as a group of well-educated boys trying to have fun and survive while at the same time keeping a smoke signal going for passing ships, degenerates into mobocracy only brought to a halt after the island is virtually set on fire and a ship with adults aboard eventually does rescue the boys before total anarchy might have set in. Ralph and Jack represent two different types of leader, a rational one in Ralph's case and the irrational Jack who develops a passionate desire to kill a pig. In what becomes almost tribal warfare between the different groups of boys, we see evidence of discrimination, torture and even murder as emotions override rules. At first, Jack is tentative about killing the pig but his growing lust for blood is highlighted when he paints his face with a clay and earthen mask behind which he loses his repressions and inhibitions, and effectively his humanity, letting out the beast within himself. In this case the mask which normally reduces the animal within us in fact allows it out with hideous consequences. It is very easy from this story to appreciate how mass hysteria can be real and can spread quickly and that without self-control we are only one step away from the "survival of the fittest" savagery of the wild animal kingdom.

The point of all this is that when faced with anxiety, guilt or inferiority, all things which can stop us from being fully human:

"…we are tempted to wear masks, to act roles. We do not trust ourselves or accept ourselves enough to be ourselves. These masks and walls are measures of self-defence, and we will live behind our walls and wear our masks as long as they are needed"

("Why am I afraid to love?" by John Powell)

Jesuit priest/psychologist Powell calls these walls ego-defence mechanisms. He reflects on the fact that the more we wear such masks the more we are merely performing as actors on a stage where there is no possibility for human growth. He also makes the salient point that we only wear these masks as long as we need them. It becomes difficult to sustain the wearing of these masks as others may at times see through them. On the football field, for example, many of us can easily see through the mask of innocence which is sometimes worn when a player has committed a particularly bad tackle and the referee is considering whether or not to send that player off the field. Similarly we may talk about those who put on a brave face at a funeral when they might wish to express their upset more openly. Of course some do, but many wear the expected mask.

In addition to the above work, John Powell wrote an equally thought-provoking title "Why am I afraid to tell you who I really am?" In that book his main contention was that if we tell others who we really are then basically that is all that we have and they may not love us. In other words our anxiety, sense of possible inferiority or guilt lead us to the conclusion that we will feel safer (for now) not revealing our true feelings and emotions as a result of which we put on emotional masks, and thus build symbolic walls to live behind, between ourselves and those we feel might not love us as our true selves.

The Phantom of the Opera has attracted millions and with good reason. This is more than the classic "good versus evil with goodness triumphant" type of story. It is a story about the tantalising desire to face our deeper self and the dangers that such a risk might unleash within us. Christine is tempted to enter the inner darkness of her soul in order to become one with the Angel of Music. Here the Phantom is potentially offering her something of a Faustian style of Devil pact in which she receives the very secret of music in order to be a truly great singer and musician while he in return receives her full commitment and very being.

What makes this story so clever is that the Phantom is not an angelic figure but a grotesque, painful character with many of the emotions he exhibits dark ones to mirror his costume. This stands in sharp contrast to Raoul who is her boyfriend and usually represented in white. However, even though Raoul endeavours to stop her talk of darkness and fears and to return to the light, the Phantom offers her an irresistible temptation from which there will be no going back to her former life including Raoul. The suggestion here is that we each have some temptation within us to dive into the deepest recesses of ourselves not only to escape the humdrum and the everyday but to expose ourselves to the danger of the darkest but possibly most thrilling secrets in us that can be unearthed. In the event Christine does flirt with the Phantom but eventually leaves him, although in one sense she has achieved a presence in both worlds.

The mask worn by the Phantom is white and stands in stark contrast to his dark costume. Why wear a mask? Here is an attempt by the Phantom to hide both physical and emotional turmoil in his life and appear as a normal person who can love and be loved. When Christine removes the mask without his agreement he is brutally exposed to his wretched past. As humans we find it hard to be truly courageous and to remove our masks and reveal our true selves for fear others will wash their hands of the real person underneath.

The complex issues of identity/masks, love, mission, redemption/salvation occur in many aspects of life, both religious and secular, and not least in our need for heroes and superheroes, often also of the masked variety. To try and understand some of the thinking here, it might be useful to consider the Classical monomyth and its counterpart the American monomyth.

In "The Hero with a Thousand Faces", first published in 1949, Joseph Campbell, in a brilliant exposition of the key tenets of comparative mythology, argues, in what we might term the Classical monomyth, for a standard cross-cultural path of mythological adventure of a hero which he describes as follows:

"A hero ventures forth from the world of common day into a region of supernatural wonder. Fabulous forces are there encountered and a decisive victory is won. The hero comes back from this mysterious adventure with a power to bestow boons (favours) on his fellow man"

Campbell uses significant heroes such as the Buddha and Moses to illustrate what he believes to be a fairly consistent pattern applicable across different cultures. We might think of many modern cinematic and literary examples.

In the American monomyth, the pattern however is slightly different:

"A community in a harmonious paradise is threatened by evil; normal institutions fail to contend with this threat; a selfless superhero emerges to renounce temptations and carry out the redemptive task; aided by fate, his decisive victory restores the community to its paradisiacal condition; the superhero then recedes into obscurity."

From Robert Jewett and John Shelton Lawrence's 1977 work "The American monomyth", the above is used to explain their view of superheroes in American culture.

Lawrence elaborates:

"The odd and the special character of the American monomyth's hero is a peculiar kind of mythic discord. Whereas most of the world's heroic myths

celebrate the social ethos of their societies, the American monomyth seems exceptional to us because it consistently dramatizes the need for its heroes to reject principles of American democracy".

When we think of superheroes in the American tradition, most of us would probably bring to mind Superman, Batman or Spiderman. Not only do they all wear masks to hide their identity, but they also have an alter ego or other identity in what we might call everyday life. Clark Kent is Superman, Bruce Wayne is Batman and Peter Parker is Spiderman. The masked superheroes have variously been described as crime fighters, masked vigilantes or saviours. Along with their strong moral codes and (usually) special powers, their masks prevent their loved ones and families from becoming targets of potential enemies/evildoers. Spiderman, with quite a broken teenage upbringing, can be a figure with whom some adolescents might identify. In one film scene he rescues a child but then evades arrest as the papers have been suggesting he is a criminal. Lawrence suggests:

"Many of the great American superstars and superhero characters have built their franchises on roles that, like Spider-Man's, show them circumventing laws and the leaders so that they can be saviours….Clint Eastwood, Mel Gibson, Sylvester Stallone, Charles Bronson, John Wayne, and many others. We find it striking that our most honoured stories and heroes are outsiders so unlike the heroes of the classical monomyth — persons who become fully integrated members of the community, accepting permanent responsibility for its welfare".

In thinking about the American monomyth, Lawrence is I think to some extent criticising democracy, suggesting that it has in some senses failed and needs to be rescued by a superhero but through the destruction of its enemies:

"The myth tells us that laws merely restrain our commitment to destroy our enemies. The American superhero is the person who understands and circumvents those laws in order to save the community or even the entire world. In our current world situation, we can see the tension between what we might call "constitutional realism" and the "call of the superhero myth"

Bruce David Forbes in his article "Religion and modern Superhero comic books" also recognises usage of religious language and imagery in some of these superhero comics and argues that even in an increasingly secular world religious languages and imagery still play a powerful role in allowing us to explore the meaning and purpose of life and thus shedding light on our attempts to make sense of it through our dreams, hopes and aspirations:

"In sum, whether comic books tell yet another apocalyptic tale of cosmic battles between good and evil, or whether they focus on the heroes' personal crises and struggles for meaning, writers and artists regularly resort to religious language and imagery to frame the stories. In addition, the deep structure of the narratives, centred round redeemer figures, seems to touch upon yearnings for deliverance. In spite of claims about secularization in modern society, and many indications of disenchantment with traditional religious institutions, the power of religious images and language remains, as a resource for humanity's grappling with questions of purpose and destiny".

I appreciate the significant difference between European and American cultures but we in Europe tend to follow many American fashions and the superhero is alive and well in our culture too I feel. The fact that we cannot all be those heroes allows us to place them on a pedestal or cloud of some sort and resort to them when the significant rips in the fabric of our lives cause us to explore some of these deeper questions in life about identity and loving and being loved more philosophically or theologically or both.

Finally, in thinking about our wearing of masks and the walls we build and hide behind by wearing them, we might also reflect on the fascinating role of the clown. Clowns for many of us can seem scary and strange. Some famous clowns in the past have assiduously painted their faces in intricate ways, depicting the smile of the entertainer whilst behind that smile lurked fragility and insecurity. It seems that comic brilliance can sometimes hide emotional hardship and even tragedy.

We only need to think of the untimely demise of comic genius Robin Williams who apparently committed suicide after suffering from extreme depression. How ironic that he had been considered for the role of Rorschach in the 2009 film Watchmen. This film made about Alan Moore and Dave Gibbons' American comic book series asked some pertinent questions about who is watching over the superheroes who are watching over us. The parallels with Robin Williams were not lost on his fans, many of whom commented on-line about an ironic joke recounted in the film by the character Rorschach. A doctor advises a depressed man to go and see the great clown Pagliacci, who happens to be in town tonight, in order to cheer himself up, but the man identifies himself to the doctor as Pagliacci! The question to ask therefore is how we are to be there for the clowns to make them laugh when <u>they</u> are depressed.

In 1970 Smokey Robinson picked up on the Pagliacci clown theme. In the song "Tears of a Clown" the subject puts on a brave face although desperately hurting inside after losing a lover. The personal struggle is obvious:

"Just like Pagliacci did, I try to keep my sadness hid, Smiling in the public eye, But in my lonely room I cry the tears of a clown when there's no one around"

So who was Pagliacci? "I Pagliacci" is in fact plural in Italian and actually refers to a "commedia del'arte" or clown troupe. The Italian opera of the name written by Leoncavallo and first performed in the 1890s is for me one of <u>the</u> world's most touching insights into the wearing of emotional masks. The opera in two acts reminds the audience at the outset that actors are real people with real feelings. The first act of the story sets up the tragedy of Canio, the troupe's lead clown (in Italian "Pagliaccio" which is the character he plays in the second act), his wife Nedda and Nedda's young lover Silvio. A second player in the troupe, Tonio makes his own advances to Nedda but they are rebuked and Tonio then reveals her infidelity with Silvio to Canio. In the second act, a play within a play in that brilliant Shakespearian tradition of Hamlet and A Midsummer Night's Dream, distinctions are blurred between the play itself and real life. The relationship tragedy is acted out with Canio/Pagliaccio, whose role as lead clown is to make the audience laugh, fighting to hold back the pain of his wife's infidelity until his emotional state makes him force Nedda to reveal her real life lover and he ends up murdering both Nedda and Silvio in his jealous anger.

Most of us want to give and receive love but are afraid of it being rejected and consequently we wear masks as walls to hide behind until we are sure that we can emerge or re-emerge as our true selves. Complexes can begin in early life, John Powell argues, and often hinge on those who love us and more crucially those who refuse to love us. He suggests that moral immaturity, caused in many cases from a lack of love, can lead to a self-centredness shown through bearing grudges and prejudices, rebellious and angry attitudes, temper tantrums and self-indulgence. These are clearly the antithesis of how genuine moral maturity might flourish. Catholic Christianity talks about twelve Fruits of the Spirit of God in charity, joy, peace, patience, kindness, goodness, generosity, gentleness, faithfulness, modesty, self-control and chastity. At the heart of any life flourishing with these can be the re-emergence of the individual from behind their walls, the building of bridges with others, the balancing of self with group, law and convention with freedom and individuality together with the subsequent removal and disposal of the now redundant masks.

In considering some of the most brutal regimes and their dictators in history, a degree of egotistical pre-occupation and narcissism must surely apply. Pol Pot, Stalin, Hitler, Chairman Mao all must bear their share of the responsibility for untold suffering and misery. Were they loved during their upbringing? Why were they afraid to show love in later years? Or could they just not remove their masks of power, control and manipulation? Powell argues that

"..in a grasping world, in a world which is gouging and clawing for the riches of this world, the Christian by his love must stand forth as a breath-taking exception".

I would argue that not merely the Christian but indeed anyone who believes in any sort of higher power or being, necessary truth or holistic humanity, should see the art of living in a similar light and try to make this world better.

This year, 2014, my wife Sue and I decided to build upon our basic knowledge and understanding of World War 2. The year celebrates and commemorates the 70th anniversary of D-Day, 6th June 1944 as well as the centenary of World War 1. At the time of writing, the stunning memorial of ceramic poppies surrounding the Tower of London marking the dead of World War 1 is gradually being removed having been sold for charity in support of those 888,246 who lost their lives in what was known as the Great War. This was supposed to be the war to end all wars though it clearly wasn't.

Neither of us claims any expertise on World War 1 but we are reasonably well informed about World War 2 and the D-day landings since we were inspired by the 70th anniversary celebrations to tour the five Normandy beaches together with connected war cemeteries in the area later on during the summer. We will, I am fairly sure, spend time on World War 1 battlefield tours too at some later stage but following the summer tour I personally am still reeling from the immensity of Operation Overlord and the events in the weeks following D-Day which we were also privileged to have explained to us and about which I admit I knew very little. I have no intention here of trying to portray Hitler as a worse dictator than any other of the many others mentioned above. That, I believe, is for a higher judge to decide. However, the facts sadly indicate that many of Hitler's dictates led to situations in which many millions of innocent people suffered and/or died.

Because this book is about what I consider to be significant and sometimes highly thought-provoking bridges and walls, I am very grateful for the opportunity within this chapter to write about what I personally believe are among the most extreme examples of each. Both feature in World War 2, namely The Atlantic Bridge (Convoy System) and the Atlantic Wall.

In writing this book, there have been many "eureka" moments for me and that in itself has made it wholly worthwhile. I always believed I had a basic level of general knowledge good enough to hold my own in quizzes and the like, but if I am honest I have developed quite a thirst for knowledge and understanding in my early 60s which allows me to marvel at the world and many of its peoples as well as being deeply saddened and hurt by it on occasions.

Socrates commented that "the unexamined life is not worth living". This is very true but in my busy working life it has been hard to find time for real learning never mind reflection. As is the case with many of us I am simply gob-smacked by the intelligence, knowledge and level of articulation shown by what I can only define as some very clever people out there. It comes to me as no surprise, then, and perhaps a little embarrassment, that I discovered how little I knew about the War in the Atlantic (and the Arctic).

The conflict known as the Battle of the Atlantic, which was Churchill's name for the conflict by around 1941, was the longest military struggle within the Second World War and lasted for its full duration from 1939 to 1945. It had its roots considerably prior to World War 1 with naval manoeuvres such as the blockade of Napoleon's fleet back in the 19th century to stop an attack on Britain. During 1939-1945, the blockading of Germany was critical in the attempt to prevent the Hitler war effort accessing resources of all types.

In 1939 it was recognised during Allied military planning that defending trade within waters close to home and the Atlantic was a top priority in order to enable Britain to import what was needed to survive and eventually to take part in the invasion plans, codenamed Neptune and Overlord, to liberate Europe from Hitler's grasp. With Italy as a leading Axis power on the German side it was also important to maintain a strong presence in the Mediterranean but this was not seen as the main priority. The Nazis claimed that a naval blockade was illegal. The battle orders sent out by the the Kriegsmarine (German Navy) in May 1939 featured the belligerent comment:

"fighting methods will never fail to be employed merely because some international regulations are opposed to them".

The German U-boat fleet together with powerful surface vessels such as the well-armed and swift Graf Spee and the Deutschland presented a threat to the Allied forces although it was widely believed that the Kriegsmarine was no match for the combined British and French naval forces in the early days of the war. The strategy of anti-submarine hunting groups proved quite ineffective against the U-Boats in that early period when nearly fifty submarines were pitched against 150 destroyers. Technology for accurately destroying submarines from the surface was still in its infancy. Hitler's Norwegian campaign of 1940 proved a set back as the firing mechanisms of the U-Boat torpedoes developed problems, although these were rectified within a year. Unfortunately during that year unescorted merchant ships were sunk with the U-boats crossing routes in "wolf packs" and it was not until 1941 that real progress was made in the development of ship borne radar. The occupation of France was similarly a setback for the Royal Navy, especially as U-Boats gained better access to the Atlantic from captured French ports. With the invasion of Norway and Denmark, France and the

Low Countries adding to pressure on Britain's fleet, the number of U-Boats was increasing as the number of Atlantic convoy escorts was decreasing.

The issue arose as to how best to protect these convoys crossing the Atlantic and returning with resources from Canada and America. It was calculated that a few large convoys with less escorts was a safer strategy than a larger number of smaller convoys with a higher ratio of escorts to merchant ships and this undoubtedly saved many lives.

Liverpool War Museum proudly tells the story as Liverpool became HQ in 1941 for Western Approaches Operations transferred from Plymouth when it became clear that ships travelling to Britain were being attacked from the German –occupied French coast ports and so were best re-routed around the northern coast of Ireland. Doenitz, U-boat Commander par excellence, discovered some weak spots on the far side of the Atlantic (where the Canadian navy were slightly weaker in numbers and experience) and south of Iceland and Greenland and he exploited these opportunities.

In spite of many setbacks, the Atlantic convoys persisted in their bravery, bringing firstly the raw materials and other goods to Britain to allow Britain to continue to withstand Hitler's advances and then later on the Canadian, American and other Allied forces to plan and prepare for the liberating invasion of Europe. However, it was not until May 1942 that what we might call a proper convoy system was in operation with 2 destroyers and 4 corvettes as convoy protection with a mixed protection fleet from UK, US and Canadian navies. It was also helpful to the protection of the convoys that Hitler had insisted on significant U-boat strength both in the Arctic and the Mediterranean and this of course meant that the German resources were scattered more thinly than they might have preferred. The development of "foxers", which were pieces of equipment towed by destroyers to divert acoustic torpedoes, similarly helped the Allied cause.

Dorothy Pederson reflects on the heroic stories of nine men in the North Atlantic in her 2005 book "Convoys of World War 2"

"*In extreme danger, they battled seasickness, injury, and less than comfortable living conditions while avoiding floating mines and torpedoes*".

I find it really humbling to even think about the watery dangers, fears, threats, sacrifices and successes of those heroes who kept supply lines open for all those years of the war.

Victory in keeping these supply lines open was achieved but at a huge cost for between 1939 and 1945 a total of 3,500 Allied merchant ships and 175 Allied warships were lost and over 70,000 Allied heroes lost their lives. Germany lost 783 U-boats with around 30,000 sailors killed.

I find the following very stirring when I think of the scale of the operations:

"....during the Atlantic Campaign only 10% of transatlantic convoys that sailed were attacked, and of those attacked only 10% on average of the ships were lost. Overall, more than 99% of all ships sailing to and from the British Isles during World War II did so successfully".

There is absolutely no doubt in my mind that the successes achieved by this Atlantic supply bridge (together with the equally brave and inspiring Arctic convoys) laid the key foundation stones without which I doubt the invasion of Europe by the Allied forces on D-Day June 6th 1944 would have ever even taken place. Especially true had Britain's resources become so weak as to cause collapse and eventual defeat.

When we turn our attention to the so-called Atlantic Wall, I have to admit that having both studied it and seen several remnants of it, the very thought of it continues to send shivers of evil down my spine.

The Battle of Britain in 1940 and especially the RAF's stubborn resistance in the air had clearly made Hitler think twice about a full invasion plan the following year and he decided instead to invade Russia on the Eastern Front. His strategy was to defeat Russia quickly (at the latest by the end of 1941) then with the massive raw material and human resources gained he would be in a far better position to invade Britain. However, the harsh Russian winter coupled with the resolve of the Russians meant that he never made it to Moscow. When the Japanese attacked Pearl Harbour, America entered the war and consequently Hitler found himself with problems on both Eastern and Western Fronts.

Deeply concerned about the increased Allied power on the Atlantic, Hitler therefore issued directives to fortify the Atlantic coastline against possible invasion from the west. From Norway down to the French/Spanish border, over 1,600 miles, this terrifying coastal defensive wall of fortifications was designed and named the Atlantikwall by Goebbels propaganda machine.

From 1942 to 1943 the main priority for Hitler was to stiffen his sea port defences but after that date the whole coastline was targeted for increased defensive capability. Not knowing which part of the coastline in France would be the most likely to be the focal point for an attack, but suspecting the Normandy beach areas less than the Calais area, the Führer, via his Commander of the Western forces General von Rundstedt, tasked leading light Erwin Rommel, the hero of North Africa, with the job.

This was a building project like no other and would eventually require the services of half a million men to guard the fortifications. Indeed to paraphrase Churchill, never had so much been built by so many and so quickly. To repel any attack from the sea effectively, it would be necessary to increase substantially the number and standard of gun emplacements along coastlines in pill boxes made out of heavily reinforced concrete. Around 15,000 concrete fortifications were ordered to be built.

A staggering total material resource of 17 million cubic metres of concrete and 1.2 million tonnes of steel was used in the whole Atlantic Wall project. Can you imagine all that delivered onto your front drive?

To stop enemy craft getting ashore, which Rommel saw as the main precursor to losing the war, beach defences needed to deliver maximum damage to possible landing vessels. If you take a typical beach defence, "Belgian grilles or gates" about 10 feet high and Maginot portcullises with mines on top were the first underwater obstacles followed by Teller mines on seaward-angled stakes, then log ramps and metal "hedgehogs", triangulated welds of pointed steel with concrete tetrahedrons again tipped with mines designed to tear the bottom off landing craft at high tide. It is widely believed that around six million mines were laid on beaches along the coast of Northern France.

Walls of barbed wire with minefields, some below and some above water level, awaited those who successfully managed to beach their landing craft, then the many aforementioned pill boxes with machine gun nests and in some places cliff top bunkers with 75-88mm guns. Shelters for U-Boats would enjoy the protection of 5 metre thick roofs, strategically important artillery batteries around 3 metres and general troop shelters just over 1 metre.

Inland were bunkers with guns in some cases up to 240mm. Low lying fields were flooded especially where Allied troops might be able to attempt landings by parachute. Not only were fields flooded but arrays of wooden spikes up to seven miles inland were set in the ground at regular intervals often topped with mines to deter landings by Allied gliders particularly near strategically important bridges. At its height during 1943, around 100 bunkers a week were being built, many using forced labour from France, Eastern Europe or North Africa. The Channel Islands which had been captured by Hitler became for him a propaganda motif for that part of Britain which was under his control and he gave orders that a twelfth of the concrete and steel used in the whole wall to be employed there. Along with those heavily fortified islands, the sea ports of Le Havre and Cherbourg and the Pas de Calais were among the best defended areas of the Wall in Northern France.

The rest was basically an unfinished structure with both significant strengths weaknesses in places, the weaknesses exploited to a large extent by the American General Dwight Eisenhower in the Normandy landings on D-Day. The Germans had certainly not underestimated the resolve of the Allies when we consider that the invasion of Europe force in total comprised some 1,200 warships, 4,000 assault craft, 1,600 merchant vessels, 13,000 aircraft and 3,500,000 troops. Eisenhower called it "the greatest amphibious assault ever attempted". Imagine the sheer planning, training and logistics management!

The Allies had chosen the Normandy beaches whilst trying to fool Hitler into believing their attack would be, as Hitler had expected, closer to Dieppe or Calais. I have seen many pieces of footage of those D-Day landings on June 6th 1944 in a wide variety of war museums. To reiterate the point I made at the start, it really sends shivers down my spine when I think how hard it must have been for those faced with a psychological wall of fear and uncertainty as well as a physical wall of unbridled horror.

For I have respectfully walked upon all five beaches, codenamed Sword, Juno, Gold, Omaha and Utah, and I can only shudder at the complete lack of protection when approaching from the sea. I am in awe at the bravery of those of all ages and particularly the young who died on the beaches or inland in subsequent battle across the fields of France and Belgium and through those towns and villages where danger lurked at every turn. I along with many others am truly humbled by their bravery and sacrifice in the cause of freedom. Some people build walls, others come to knock them down. Their act ostensibly done from a sense of duty was, I argue, truly an act of immeasurable love.

Chapter 4   The "isms"

"The biblical account of Noah's Ark and the Flood is perhaps the most implausible story for fundamentalists to defend. Where, for example, while loading his Ark did Noah find penguins and polar bears in Palestine?"

Judith Hayes

In the summer of 1996, I decided to take the family to Israel. At that time although I had already been in the world of work for twenty years, I had been teaching Religious Education for only a couple of years. Naturally I thought that a fuller knowledge and understanding of Jewish history and culture would be helpful in my teaching, especially at A-Level as we used to teach a module on the Old Testament of the Bible. I also hoped it would allow Sue and my two sons, Chris and Rob, a unique opportunity to visit some of the key sites in the Judaeo-Christian and Islamic traditions. I had planned for it to be as much a holiday as a pilgrimage. It had been relatively peaceful in Israel and the immediately surrounding countries that year so I went for it. I presumed that we would be with a pilgrimage crowd for some parts of the week but hoped we could have our personal space as a family to enjoy the holiday in other ways too.

We had spent the first night in a hotel at Netanya on the coast as per the schedule and awaited contact from the tour guide the next morning. When he phoned me I was really gobsmacked to learn that we were the only people in the party and not only that but he (Miron) would drive us around in our very own minibus and take us basically wherever we wanted over the week. Of course we did all the usual sites in Bethlehem, Nazareth and Jerusalem. I had, however, planned what I particularly fancied seeing and so we went off track at times, for example to the Golan Heights in the north and the more likely site for the Good Samaritan inn off the beaten track south of Jerusalem. How lucky I was to have my own personal expert on hand to try and answer all my many questions (teachers ask a lot!). Miron had years of experience and had shown all manner of people around from Heads of State downwards so he really knew his subject. I would describe him as a liberal Jew, certainly no fundamentalist, which suited me well because he would present tradition brilliantly but would often have his own take on meanings and symbolism as indeed have I in my own Catholic faith.

No visit to Israel would be complete without a visit to the Dead Sea, the lowest point on the earth, and to Jericho, a city many believe to be the oldest on the planet. We had our swim, or more correctly our float, in the salty Dead Sea and needed a good shower to wash that burning saltiness off our skin.

Jericho was the hottest place I had visited at that time in my life. When the temperature is in the mid-forties Centigrade all you want to do is sit in the shade and drink water! Nevertheless Miron showed us one of the oldest man-made structures on earth, the base of the watchtower as part of the walled fortifications of Jericho. The watchtower is believed to be from the pre-pottery Neolithic Age which suggests a possible construction date of sometime around 8,000BC. This was incredibly old! I could hardly believe I was looking down at this ancient watchtower of Jericho's fortifications with about 9,000 or 10,000 years of history between us.

This chapter is entitled "The isms". According to Webster's dictionary an "ism" is a "distinctive doctrine, system or theory" (Google includes "philosophy").

The Phrontistery (from Greek phroneein, to think) quotes a list of 234 major "isms" although other sites list more than 800. From Absolutism via Communism, Existentialism, Globalism, Hedonism, Secularism and Utilitarianism to Zootheism, to mention only a few, there are all manner of such philosophies, doctrines and ideologies in society. If I highlight only a handful, that I feel will be more than enough of a task.

Among all the "isms" for me one of the most thought-provoking is Fundamentalism. I studied avidly Malise Ruthven's excellent work on the search for the meaning of the word in its many different contexts. This problematical term needs to include discussions around literalism, traditionalism, integralism, nationalism and ethnicity if one is to have developed a fuller and deeper understanding of the term. Ruthven argues intelligently by working through each of these concepts and attempts where appropriate connecting them to Wittgenstein's concept of family resemblances, suggesting that just as similarities overlap in complex ways among family units, so it is with the fundamentalist concept across religious and secular societies.

This helps us to see how fundamentalism involves shared themes across the globe such as a narrower interpretation of scripture and its purpose, the use of violence, gender issues and group identities to preserve at all costs the authentic nature of celestial messages. American fundamentalism in Southern California of the early 1900s provides some early roots for the term we use today, especially in the sponsorship, by Milton and Lyman Stewart in 1910, of publications known as "The Fundamentals". Key areas for the American fundamentalists, whose denominational diversity grew in large part due to Thomas Jefferson's "wall of separation between Church and State", were the infallibility of Scripture, the incarnation of Christ and the Virgin birth, Jesus's death as atonement for sin, the physical resurrection from the dead and Jesus's actual return in the Second Coming at the end of time. The scriptural aspect is particularly interesting as freedom from error (or inerrancy as it came to be called) is arguably different from pure literalism, the former being its purity and reliability as the word of God, the latter being open to pitfalls arising from the fact that an understanding of scriptural texts in their literal rather than symbolic sense as Ruthven argues "opens those very flood gates of textual criticism to which those fundamentalists are most adamantly opposed".

The physical walls of the parts of ancient Jericho that we had been shown are an apt topic for a debate between those two religious "isms", Biblical fundamentalism with its focus on factual and/or historical accuracy and Biblical symbolism with its regard for the insights the stories gives us of God and our relationship as humans with God.

"Joshua fit (fought) the battle of Jericho and the walls came a-tumbling down" say the lyrics of the well-known African-American Spiritual.

In the Old Testament in Joshua 6 we are told that God said to Joshua:

"See, I have delivered Jericho into your hands, along with its king and fighting men. March around the city once with all the armed men. Do this for six days. Have seven priests carry trumpets of rams' horns in front of the ark. On the seventh day, march around the city seven times, with the priests blowing the trumpets. When you hear them sound a long blast on the trumpets, have the whole army give a loud shout; then the wall of the city will collapse and the army will go up, everyone straight in." (Bible NIV)

Did the wall(s) fall literally/historically down or was the writer using symbolic imagery to show God's power here?

Site excavations were carried out in the 1950s under the auspices of British archaeologist Kathleen Kenyon who summarised thus:

'It is a sad fact that of the town walls of the Late Bronze Age, within which period the attack by the Israelites must fall by any dating, not a trace remains …. The excavation of Jericho, therefore, has thrown no light on the walls of Jericho of which the destruction is so vividly described in the Book of Joshua.'

Bryant Wood, creationist archaeologist and Research Director of the Inerrant Associates for Biblical Research in 1990, concluded quite differently (from much of Kenyon's own archaeological evidence) suggesting that she had misdated the destruction of Jericho at about 1550BC. He argues that it took place around 1400BC which he took to be in accord with the Bible account.

He postulated that after the seventh march around the city on the seventh day, at the part where the Biblical account says the wall fell flat, it in fact *"fell beneath itself"*…as a result of its design of retaining wall, embankment and mud brick wall. He believed that there was very convincing factual /historical evidence that the mud brick wall collapsed and fell to the base of the stone retaining wall. He argued that Kenyon's detailed work had in effect found a heap of bricks from the fallen wall of Jericho city.

Wood concluded:

"The archaeological evidence supports the historical accuracy of the Biblical account in every detail. Every aspect of the story that could possibly be verified by the findings of archaeology is, in fact, verified".

From a fundamentalist standpoint, the walls may indeed have fallen as the Bible indicates, but as I used to say to my students I was not around with a digital camcorder at the time so it might be wise to keep an open-minded approach!

The quote on the topic of Noah's Ark at the head of this chapter offers just as much of a challenge to the historically/factually driven Biblical fundamentalist. Many of those who view the Noah's Ark story from a symbolic perspective would ask instead what the story means and what it is trying to encourage us to explore about our relationship with God using the key themes in the story such as sin, punishment, consequences, hope, promises and salvation.

Literalist fundamentalists, those who take the Bible text as a factually true account, letter by letter, might well still be on the top of Mount Ararat in Turkey hunting for Noah's Ark as you read this, since legend points out that very mountain top as the most likely site for the eventual landing place of the Ark after the Flood had subsided. Those who view the story symbolically might argue that a wooden Ark of the size mentioned in Genesis would have been impossible to construct or sail without steel bulkheads to stop water pressures causing implosion. In addition they would question, as the chapter heading quote does, just how Noah managed to get two of every living creature together. Did he have to go and collect them or did the creatures present themselves voluntarily? How long might all that have taken? Was there even enough water vapour in the atmosphere or in the deeps to completely drown the earth to the requisite depth as is suggested by the story?

Other Biblical fundamentalists may yet be searching in modern Iraq for the Garden of Eden. Liberals might ask instead what the Garden means. To a desert people, the Garden which God created for Adam and Eve would have represented an oasis in a desert culture, a paradise on earth.

I recall an African story we used to use about a hungry hyena torn in his choice of two paths when he smells food. He sniffs to the left and then to the right but ends up so vexed that he tries to go in both directions and tears himself in two. I would ask the students if the story was true/really happened. Most said no, of course it was not true. Some said it was but not factually. Then what was the point of it? They explained that the story was trying to teach us that greed kills, and that the hyena was in fact a symbol crafted by the author to use as a vehicle for this main teaching message.

We concluded that, from a symbolic perspective anyway, a good question to ask in the case of many Bible stories, when thinking about the culture in which they were written, was not whether they are true or not but rather what do they teach us of God and what type of truths do they contain?

Of course many fundamentalists could be unhappy with this symbolic interpretative way of thinking but would argue that the events happened exactly as recorded (especially literalists) and many fundamentalists would argue that if there were inconsistencies, there remains more for us to find out yet but the stories are still true (factual/historical truth). There would be some stories with historical facts for definite, of course, such as the histories of some of the Jewish Kings which even liberals would be quite likely to accept as true in a factual/historical sense. This is always going to be a controversial area, as evidenced by scholars such as Jewish scholar Isaac ibn Yashush who noted in the eleventh century, for example, that the list of Kings in Genesis 36 included some who lived for a long time after Moses was believed to have died (Moses was believed originally to have written the first five books of the Bible known as the Pentateuch).

In an excellent article "A discourse on isms and the principle of sharing", Mohammed Mesbahi, of STWR (Share the World's Resources) points out that a broader range of "isms" in society than purely religious ones have led us to be

"confused, fearful and complacent"

as we have been conditioned by them. Only

"when there is a material basis for trust and security in society alongside a universal teaching in the Laws of Life, there will be no further need for people to identify with and proliferate the manifold isms in all their forms".

He argues that the conditioning we have received through theses "isms" has led us to a

"spiritual blindness as to the true reality of life".

Some isms can be said to be relatively harmless or even beneficial. For example, holism is the concept of the interconnectedness of things in the universe, objectivism argues reality exists outside the mind and tychism is the idea of accepting the idea of pure chance. However, Mesbahi thinks others

"are manipulated for the purposes of power and control, especially in the fields of education, religion and politics".

He talks about how *"isms pervade everywhere around us which means that we ourselves live from within these isms. It is not 'I think, therefore I am', as the philosopher Descartes said, but rather 'I believe, therefore I am.'*

This has apparently led us to a situation in which we cannot be truly who we are supposed to be because:

"in a society that is subjugated by innumerable isms and beliefs, it almost appears as if humanity's favorite pastime is to be anxious and afraid, albeit unconsciously and often without due reason".

This in turn, he argues, leads us into thinking from a position not of how things really are but of how (based on the isms which we have been brought up with) they should be. Examples of how this has damaged us include our inability to *"live in the moment, to appreciate the beauty of life without naming it, to experience a quiescence of thought that is not constantly measuring, comparing and projecting images."*

It is arguably not the beliefs of the isms themselves which are the real danger but the adherence to belief systems which are about wrong identification. From atheism he gives the example of an atheist which as a label he terms "divisive" and "violent" because:

"the atheist cannot exist without an opposing set of beliefs in God, and where there is division there is also violence – of an intellectual or psychological if not of a physical nature".

He also suggests that:

"Capitalism is now a lonely boy who won the war of isms in the end, which is largely because the infringement of free will in capitalist societies is far more covert and marginalised " (than in, for example, Communism or Marxism).

Some isms have led to extreme persecution and destruction. The Western Wall of the Jerusalem Temple is a case in point when looking at Roman Imperialism. When we stood there back in 1996, with Sue on the other side of a dividing wall (fence actually) in the women's section, we marveled at this remnant of the mighty Herod's Temple, little knowing about the true carnage that had happened there two thousand years ago.

Mount Moriah is a hill in the old part of the city of Jerusalem where Abraham, the father of Judaism, is believed to have been willing to sacrifice his son Isaac and where the Dome of the Rock stands with its beautiful roof as one of the most holy sites in Islam. The total area of Temple Mount is assessed at over one million square feet so Herod's Temple must have been really impressive.

King Solomon had built the first Jerusalem Temple there, finished in 957BC. Nebuchadnezzar of Babylon destroyed it in 586 BC, but it was rebuilt by 515 BC. King Herod enlarged it and the famous Western Wall (the "Wailing Wall") was built which is the only physical remains of the Temple. For in 70 AD, Jerusalem was besieged and the Temple destroyed leaving only the Western Wall standing. Some argue that it was a gesture to leave this small part by the Romans to show their might and power, others suggest it was simply not that important to the Romans and so it was left alone. I realise now that the massacre of the inhabitants of the city and its immediate surrounds was as brutal as any we have witnessed in history. In

"The Wars of the Jews" the historian Josephus claims that over one million were killed during the siege, mostly Jews, and some 97,000 were captured and made slaves.

In the "History of the Jews" book 16 (Milman) it records that

"The slaughter within was even more dreadful than the spectacle from without. Men and women, old and young, insurgents and priests, those who fought and those who entreated mercy, were hewn down in indiscriminate carnage. The number of the slain exceeded that of the slayers. The legionaries had to clamber over heaps of dead to carry on the work of extermination."

Jews were not allowed back into Jerusalem until Byzantine times, when they were allowed just once a year on the anniversary of the destruction of the Temple and many would naturally weep over the ruins of the Holy Temple. No wonder that their remnant of their Herod's Temple became known as the "Wailing Wall." This remains their most holy site and it is very clear to see why.

For further scenarios of persecution and destruction, whilst on the subject of Imperialism and Nationalism, I now turn to modern Israel and Palestine. During our 1996 visit, Miron told us a great deal about the creation of the State of Israel and the Palestinian question.

If fundamentalism needs to include aspects of nationalism and ethnicity, as Ruthven claims, then the reasons for Middle Eastern tensions arising from World War 1 and subsequent events in that area leading to current conflicts and terrorism in the regions become much clearer. During the course of World War 1, the secretive "Sykes-Picot agreement" was reached between Britain and France that should the Ottoman Empire be defeated the at the end of the war, the Arab states of that Empire would be divided between Britain and France for control and administration. Sir Mark Sykes and François Georges-Picot were the diplomats responsible for the negotiation of this agreement. At the end of the war, France took responsibility for Syria and Lebanon while Britain took responsibility for Mesopotamia (now Iraq) and Palestine (now Jordan and Israel). Whilst some of these countries became independent in future years, Palestine was an on-going problem, particularly after World War 2 when Arab Nationalism was on the rise.

In 1947 a plan was drawn up by the United Nations Palestine Committee which would lead to the division of Palestine into Arab and Jewish states. The expectation was that these could co-exist. Hostilities unfortunately followed the acceptance of the plan by the Jews but its rejection by the Arabs.

In 1948 the State of Israel was created as the British mandate for control ran out. The creation of this State left Arabs bitter and many were forced to leave their own towns or cities and settle in the area on the western bank of the river Jordan. Jordan now had control of this West Bank territory while the Gaza region (in Old Testament times the land of Goliath and the Philistines) came under Egyptian control and the rest of Western Palestine was the new State of Israel's territory.

In a war lasting only six days in 1967, Israel took back the West Bank from Jordan, the Gaza strip from Egypt and the Golan Heights (that most northerly bit we visited) from Syria. It was ordered to withdraw from those territories by the United Nations and did so apart from keeping East Jerusalem and the Golan Heights.

A State of Palestine was declared in 1988 by the Palestinian National Council, part of the Palestinian Liberation Organisation (PLO). In 2012 Palestine was given an upgrade in status to "non-member observer state" by the United Nations. Plans are still being debated today by Palestinian Authorities for a future full State of Palestine with a capital of East Jerusalem and encompassing the West Bank and Gaza strip. This is complex for a variety of reasons, not the least of which is the on-going dispute over the 1949 agreements on just what territory the West Bank includes.

Despite various peace process attempts little has been resolved. This is hardly surprising considering, for example, the two diametrically opposed views of Gush Emunim, the Bloc of the Faithful, who are Zionists looking at the need for the whole of Israel (including the disputed secular state and the Palestinian territories captured in the Six day war) to be held in trust until the Messiah comes, and the Haredim groups who do not even accept the State of Israel and stick strictly to religious legal orthodoxy.

Around 1992 a physical wall to separate Israel from Palestine was suggested by Israeli Prime Minister Yitzhak Rabin, ultimately assassinated after signing Oslo peace accords with Yasser Arafat, Chairman of the Palestine Liberation Organisation. By 2012, more than two-thirds of it was completed or under construction with slightly less than a third still to be started. Israel's desire for having this wall was to reduce and ideally stop suicide bombings and other attacks on Israeli territory. It appears that where the wall has been erected this has tended to happen. Israelis claim it is helping Palestinians as there are less security checkpoints and restrictions.

However, for many Palestinians this has been seen as imprisonment in their own territory with a significant reduction in their freedom and significant loss of land where Israel has arguably built the wall to its own advantage. In fact there are claims that up to one tenth of the Palestinian territory has been taken back by Israel due to the lines of the wall varying from the 1949 demarcation agreements or "Green Line " as it was known. Many comments have been made by a whole range of bodies on this issue. Churches and Human Rights organisations have criticised the abuses of Human Rights due to the building of the wall. Some such as the Organisation of the Islamic Conference call it a

"crime of apartheid".

Michael Cohen in the article "Israel's cult of Securitism" talks about a current glorification of security and army. He suggests that their defence forces get a much higher rating in popularity votes than other social institutions. He thinks that such popularity is turning the country into a "garrison state" with a deeply engrained "siege mentality". I suggest the roots may lie within events such as the destruction of various Temples throughout their history and the scattering of Jewish believers all over the world (known as the Diaspora). The need to protect and maintain a strong border including the unfinished wall between Israel and Palestine in the West Bank and Gaza strip regions has possibly made Israel even more aware of its geographically crucial location.

This idea of "Securitism" is not only confined to Israel, but is manifest in a slightly less military fashion but possibly one smacking even more of elitism and egoism in others areas of the world. I refer to the practice of enhancing home security to a hitherto unimaginable level. For some years now there have been companies offering managed security solutions to private or public sector bodies keen to protect against cyber terrorism in its many chameleon-like forms.

The complexity of data systems has for several years called for some of the very brightest minds to counteract inappropriate attempts at access by careful monitoring of data patterns in order to identify anomalies early and implement timely and appropriate counter-measures. Some top-end properties of the exceedingly rich and worried have become veritable fortresses in their own right. From rooftop helipads to steel encased safe core/panic rooms and cellars dug deep into rock built to withstand nuclear standard blasts, such homes boast ultra-sensitive heat-sensing equipment to identify intruders from a great distance. Coupled with this are heating, water and air filtration systems capable of ensuring owner survival within their walls when faced with sophisticated attacks from without.

"Walled gardens" of a different breed and type which would be quite incomprehensible to the Selfish Giant are originally the idea of John Malone whose company was ultimately bought by communications "giant" AT and T just before the turn of the century. Apple has specialised in this area for some time and the iOS platform used on iPads and iPhones is in effect a walled garden of software which is in theory safe against viruses. School exam boards use walled gardens as a matter of course. The contents of the "garden" are accessible only to those who have been provided with a special password or sets of passwords and identification methods over and above the passwords and registration arrangements often need to surf the site in question. In other words, even though others may access most of the same website for other information, the specific contents of the walled garden are protected from anyone viewing or sharing them other than those authorised by the garden passwords.

This concept certainly does not please everyone but is extremely useful for those organisations who wish to offer restricted content to a limited and closely monitored pool of users. Some would argue, for example, that walled gardens stop those who release software from freely distributing it as well as restricting the freedom of the user. It is felt in some quarters that walled gardens have already created unwelcome monopolies for some of the most powerful software providers. We might speculate that iOS hidden tethering has meant that unlike the odd hole in the wall which already existed and through which the children managed to get back into the Selfish Giant's garden, with some software providers it might take a Humpty Dumpty siege engine to break down those walls!

One of the most beautiful and breath-taking bridges I have visited was in Mostar, part of the former Yugoslavia. In order to explain the powerful symbolism of this bridge's history, I should firstly explain some of the background to the Yugoslav Wars and the "isms" which took place between 1991 and 1999.

Yugoslavia has always had a fascination for me. Slavic football teams often boasted talented ball players combined with a toughness that made them difficult to beat in international competitions. Perhaps some of this came from the Tito era. Yugoslavia was created after World War 1. It was a nation mainly of Christian Slavs but with many Muslims alongside.

After World War 2 the new Socialist Federal Republic was set up under Josip Tito who ran the country under an authoritarian style of leadership but up until his death in 1980 was seen as a benevolent Communist and was generally well thought of at home and abroad. He succeeded in maintaining a unity during his Presidency from 1953. However, after his death the relationships he had skilfully maintained between the six republics of Slovenia, Croatia, Bosnia-Hercegovina, Serbia (which included Vojvodina and Kosovo), Montenegro and Macedonia began to disintegrate.

Nationalism was in the ascendancy. The Yugoslav People's Army (JNA) was expected to continue representing the entire nation as it had done under its former appearance as the People's Liberation Army of Yugoslavia. Serbia, led by Slobodan Milosevic, manoeuvred itself into a commanding position within the Federation of holding four out of the full eight presidency votes. The Seperatists Croatia and Slovenia declared independence in 1991. This led the then Yugoslavian Prime Minister Markovic to veto their breakaways and offer his support to the JNA as a means of keeping the country from falling apart. After a partially successful attempt by the JNA to stop the Slovenians leaving the Federation, a four year War of Independence took place in Croatia during which the JNA sided with Croatian Serb rebels. Serbian and Monenegrin forces attacked. Milosovic wanted to create a Greater Serbia.

Even the Croatian jewel of the Adriatic, the unique UNESCO heritage site of Dubrovnik, was shelled. We had visited Dubrovnik in 1990 just before the war. I remember standing on the mountain above the town on a play area with Chris and Rob looking out at the becalmed and pearly Adriatic which I still believe was the closest I have been to heaven on this earth. The view over the town and out to sea was simply stunning. How sad it was that only a year later, that same mountain top would be an artillery base used in the shelling of a priceless treasure.

From 1992 to 1995 the conflict spread beyond Croatia to Bosnia-Herzegovina which was a real flashpoint as it was probably culturally the most mixed of the six original republics with relations between Muslims, Catholics and Orthodox particularly strained. The siege of its capital Sarajevo was the longest of any city in the modern world, a siege lasting from April 1992 to February 1996. Bosnian Serbs surrounded it from the hillsides with 13,000 soldiers and it took a merciless pounding resulting in the deaths of more than the attacking force. I particularly remember footage night after night on the news about the massacre of Srebrenica, a Bosnian Muslim enclave. This was probably an attempt at genocide though up until to now the courts have not accepted it as such. Over 5,000 men and boys were arguably ethnically cleansed by the Bosnian Serb Army (Republika Srpska) under Ratko Mladic. Eventually Mladic's trial for war crimes opened in The Hague in 2012.

This brings me to Stari Most which I visited in 1989, the year previous to taking the family to Dubrovnik and two years previous to the start of the wars. Stari Most or Old Bridge is the name of a truly stunning bridge ordered to be constructed in 1557 by Muslim Emperor Suleiman the Magnificent via Hajrudin, a student of Sinan, Suleiman's chief architect. The bridge spanned the fast flowing river Neretva in the lovely Old Town of Mostar. If the Great Wall of China was held together with rice mortar, then Stari Most was held together with the protein of egg whites. At 4 metres wide and 28 metres long, this bridge stood 20 metres high. Famous 17th century traveller Çelebi said that

"the bridge is like a rainbow arch soaring up to the skies, extending from one cliff to the other. I, a poor and miserable slave of Allah, have passed through 16 countries, but I have never seen such a high bridge. It is thrown from rock to rock as high as the sky".

Mostar had for a long time been a cosmopolitan city with considerable ethnic diversity. The river Neretva at Stari Most had been a physical divide for a Croat/Catholic community on the Western side and a Bosniak/Muslim community on the Eastern side of the river.

I recall a steep climb up, then a steep incline down slippery marbled slabs when crossing this arched bridge. Athletic young men would dive off the very top of the bridge into the river below for a generous donation.

During the hostilities in Bosnia-Herzegovina came a brutal act which for me was both deeply upsetting and hugely outrageous. This beautiful heritage bridge was shelled and destroyed in November 1993. Stari Most had been hit many times for over a year but eventually succumbed to somewhere in the region of 60 shells on one November day. The rationale given by the Bosnian Croats was that it was strategically significant, but it is also possible that it was an act of revenge on cultural property in order to make a point. It trapped more than 20,000 Bosnian Muslims on the east bank of the river and even cut off a major supply of drinking water on what was then a front line of battle.

In the next two chapters I will be exploring why I believe human nature is not all bad. However, I intend to start right now. Stari Most, which had become a cultural centrepiece and a symbol for tolerance of diversity in Mostar, was wonderfully restored after the war. A multinational force, SFOR, was set up to stabilise the region and had a major hand in the reconstruction. A financial team including representation from the World Bank and UNESCO pulled in countries such as Turkey, Croatia and Italy to fund the reconstruction plans which were going to cost in excess of US$12million.

Er-Bu, a Turkish construction company with a track record in bridge repairs, was contracted and used Ottoman construction methods and materials as close to the original as was possible. Working under the shadows of destroyed mosques, walls and houses which had been pummelled by mortar attacks and machine gun bullets on that eastern bank, Hungarian Army divers succeeded in recovering most of the original stones from the bottom of the fast-flowing Neretva, often in dangerous conditions. Reconstruction commenced in 2001 and the bridge was spectacularly re-opened by UNESCO in 2004. This was about far more than simply re-building a monument, even though memory of the original 10 year work of Hajrudin became a huge factor. This was even more than a restoration of Mostar's buildings on either side of its picturesque cobbled-streets. It was no less than a powerful and symbolic reconciliation of communities which had been split apart by the war.

Fundamentalism in its broader sense certainly has its critics as have many of the isms. So what exactly is the opposite of a fundamentalist? In a web blog musing about education, democracy and the current state of affairs in the USA, Eileen Good struggled to find an antonym for fundamentalism. She found plenty of synonyms such as

… "*extremist, fanatic, intransigent, reactionary, zealot…*"

She contended that the best antonym was "educated". She went on to explain that educated people can address problems from multiple angles, and from that range are able to choose the best strategy or solution in a given situation using creative thinking and researching possible alternatives. She argued that these solutions in terms of beliefs must be tempered by research and investigation and must be modified as the thinking develops. Educated people do this. Furthermore the educated person will be tolerant of the thinking and belief systems of others. This type of thinking, I believe, is going to become highly important in a world in which terrorism is currently forming a significant threat to the peace and stability of our planet.

Chapter 5   Liberation
"I'm free to be whatever I……"

(Oasis)

The great sports stars are very much in the entertainment business. Since many tickets are expensive, it seems obvious that we need value for money. But whilst entertainment is very important and without it most fan bases will fall away to some extent over time, nevertheless it is often seen, at least in professional sport, that winning is the important thing. I take the point, because if your team is winning you will go and watch them to see, not only that they are picking up trophies, but that they are also playing with some style. However, if they are on a bad losing streak you may still find the die-hard supporters there chanting "United/City till I die" but you won't find many "fair weather" supporters very often, even in the fairest of weather.

Some individuals and teams I talked about in Chapter 1 are resolute by nature. They play a tough game and defence is their priority. It always has been and it always will be. This is sensible to a degree, as especially towards the semi-finals and finals of many sporting competitions, many games tend to tighten up as no-one wants to lose. At the top level of Test cricket, you won't get very far without a solid defence when batting. At that level of the game the bowlers are able to spot or work out very quickly any weaknesses in your batting and they frequently do. Consequently if you are intending to build a century and contribute to winning the game, it takes time and patience as well as large amounts of concentration. In top flight snooker it is much the same. You need to be all to play all the shots but unless you can stay the course by defending well with good positional safety play you are highly unlikely ever to win a major tournament.

The same goes for tennis. Djokovic, Federer, Nadal and Murray can all play the most exquisite of attacking shots but they know when to play them and they have the knack of selecting the correct defensive shot at the right time until they can work a position from which to go out and attack to win the point. On those crucial break and set points this becomes even more important. Again, patience and doggedness pay off. In football, there are mixed opinions about whether it is best to play brilliant, entertaining football or to play a strong defensive game, and of course you really need to be able to do both if you want to win finals and attract large, appreciative crowds who want to see more, as with any entertainment that is enjoyable. The top teams tend to keep things tight, though, because one slip, one defensive lapse in concentration and you get punished by the better teams. One mistake may be all it takes since the other team, having scored, are then able to shut up shop themselves and no matter how hard you try, they frequently manage to keep their shape and discipline so that scoring an equaliser may prove, for your team, a bridge too far.

One reason why some of the top stars are paid so well and respected so highly is that they possess the magic key to unlock this situation, especially on the biggest stages. In football, playing with the full width of the pitch allows top players extra capacity to get round the back of the defence, put defenders on the back foot or end up facing the wrong way so they are pulled out of their tight defensive shape. A skilfully worked free kick against the very best of defensive walls can still find the net. Just as the children found a gap in the Selfish Giant's garden wall, Cristiano Ronaldo and Lionel Messi know how to find the gap at the bottom of the spray-can-marked defensive wall near its edge, or they are able to fire it point blank through the wall knowing that a defender might just move a fraction and that their pinpoint accuracy will be enough.

The problem with walls is that sometimes they are just too solidly constructed and, having failed to engineer the sort of gap I have just mentioned, the only way for the true free kick specialist to beat the wall is to go over it or round it. The free kick specialists are heroic in their ability to swerve the ball outside the line of the wall and suddenly drift the ball back in to find the top corner of the net. Or the ball (and this is an exceptional piece of skill) is directed over the top in such a way that it comes down very quickly from its trajectory and before the defenders in the wall realise it the ball is sailing past them and nestling in the net rather than in row Z .The more average player does tend to put it into row Z (though hopefully a much lower row) several times before getting closer to the goalposts or bar!

The Ronaldo and Messi magic can beat the wall in whichever way is needed although no one ever said it was easy and they certainly would not, even though they make it look easy. Just think how many hours are spent on the tennis court by the top players practising their defensive forehand or backhand over and over again, the most belligerent of batsmen push-ing quietly down the line of the ball time and again or the snooker genius getting the cue ball so tight to the cushion that his opponent is forced into an error from which he or she can then clean up the table in what seems like an instant. All based on graft and patience. Genius, as many of us have been taught, is far more perspiration than inspiration.

We believe defences are there to be opened up or destroyed. It is one of our most basic human instincts and behaviours to want to be victorious and ultimately free, perhaps in the sporting sense free to lift the trophy. In life this often means that whichever wall is placed in our way, unless it is offering us the protection or safety we seek or are enjoying, we will try to find a way to beat that wall. Physically, intellectually, socially, psychologi-cally, spiritually, it makes little difference. We will keep trying until we find a way or we may be willing to die in the attempt. Many have been. Even the sleeping man, on waking up in his locked room, believed himself to be free.

Havel's prison walls which I mentioned earlier give inmates ample time to think and to reflect, which can be a dangerous thing to do with human beings. In the early part of "The Great Escape", (put up your hand and stand in the corner if you have been away every Christmas and Easter for the last twenty years and have still not seen it!) it seems obvious that many escapes had already been planned in concentration camps across Europe and that the triple tunnel plan to build Tom, Dick and Harry was really just a continuation of these.

Before embarking on the certain dangers of tunnelling out, prisoners would firstly have tried to escape by using the existing "escape facilities" or opportunities kindly provided by their captors such as hiding themselves in laundry baskets or bales of hay or refuse bins, or failing this tying them-selves to the undercarriages of trucks and waiting to be driven out of the gates of the prison in a relatively comfortable and cost-effective way! Plans of that nature relied very heavily on the apathy or lethargy of the drivers and guards. Occasionally checks on the many goods and service vehicles entering or leaving prisons were not done as thoroughly as they should have been and so some inmates escaped. More often than not, however, the ingenious methods employed were in reality not quite as ingenious as the would-be escapees thought and in any event were fully to be expected and must therefore be anticipated at every turn by any Commandant worthy of the name. It certainly made good sense for the Commandant to make an example of those who had tried to escape but had been recaptured and this could be anything from a few discouraging days in solitary confinement (memories of Steve McQueen with his baseball kit in the "cooler") to hanging or shooting in a public display to deter any one else from being so foolhardy in the future. However, as I suggested before, the indomitable human spirit will not be imprisoned and is more than a match for all this. I suspect some Commandants must have been dumbstruck by the sheer boldness, persistence, creativity and doggedness of many of those who never stopped trying.

The camp on which the film "The Great Escape" was based was Stalag Luft 3, now in modern Poland near Sagan, but at the time this area was called Lower Silesia in Germany. The area was chosen specifically because of yellowish sandy, crumbly soil which would stand out against the greyish soil of the compound. Additionally, huts were raised well off the ground to aid detection of possible tunnels. Some attempts by the Germans at using sound basis detecting equipment were also in evidence.

The audacious plan hatched by Squadron Leader Roger Bushell of the RAF was to build the three tunnels Tom, Dick and Harry at the same time and to get over 200 men out. The assumption was that the Germans, if they discovered one of the tunnels, would not believe that there could possibly be two more. The tunnels were started under drains and stoves to avoid being obvious. It was hard work digging and was, of course, done in shifts. Breathable air was difficult to obtain and pumps were manufactured from all manner of objects to ensure the diggers did not suffocate, especially given that the tunnel, though some 30 feet deep, was only a couple of feet wide and liable to collapse at any time due to that soft sandy soil. Over 600 men worked on the tunnels although many of them had to draw lots to see if they would feature in the final escape team of 200.

As the film shows, soil was cleverly stored in long bags made of stockings around the shoulders and down the legs inside trench coats and was sprinkled onto the compound in gardening areas and kicked about or mixed with the grey soil on the compound's surface. Timbers to shore up the tunnels were mainly removed from bunk beds along with a whole range of other materials (some of which was stolen from German stores or from bribed guards) such as pillows, electric cable/wire, tables, spoons and forks and blankets.

Given the massive scale of materials used on the tunnels and the fact that the Germans continuously suspected things were going on, it is remarkable they did not find all three tunnels. Two of the tunnels were discovered and work had to stop on the remaining tunnel Harry for a few months. Eventually the plan was put into operation and in a moonlight escape, 76 men got out before the plan was discovered. This in itself was astonishing since the tunnel had come up outside of the perimeter defences but short of the relative safety of the woods. In addition the weather was bad with ice and snow. The Germans recaptured 73 out of the 76. About half were executed.

We all like to "escape" our walls from time to time. There are programmes on television in which couples, often wishing to leave an urban sprawl and search for their dream property in a rural setting, are given various properties to consider. Depending on the couple's budget, the features and benefits of these properties are shown to the couple who are given the opportunity to critique each and say at the end of the show whether they would consider making an offer on any of them. Sometimes this happens, but often it does not. Sometimes the desirable properties are in more exotic locations with warmer climates many miles from here.

An interesting psychology is in evidence here. Why talk of "escape"? It is hardly equal that from Stalag Luft 3. I could be controversial here and ask how this type of escapism differs from the type some strive to achieve by taking drugs of various kinds. When I was doing drug education at school I always made a point of explaining that people have taken stimulants and anti-depressants for centuries and that the temptations were not something radically new to their generation. Drugs are of course medicines and I would argue they always need to be taken under proper medical prescription. At the same time, of course, there are drugs which are taken by nearly all of us such as caffeine. The point I would make about escapism is that we all do it to an extent. While some search for properties in remote locations, others search for a holiday on a deserted island, or on some piece of forest where human feet have never trodden. Others, wishing to escape the crowds, seem quite content to read a book on a quiet campsite. Yet others try to find some escape through the use of substances. It is quite possible that all may end up pleased or disappointed. I suppose you can't really blame people for trying to find the level of freedom which they themselves believe will ensure happiness. You certainly would not wish me to tell you what to do or how to behave any more than I would wish you to admonish my own morality. I like philosopher John Stuart Mill's libertarian approach to socially acceptable behaviour which argues that the point at which it becomes anti-social is the point at which you start to infringe other people's liberty.

Isambard Kingdom Brunel's beautifully engineered suspension bridge over the gorge of the river Avon at Clifton in Bristol recently celebrated its 150th anniversary with massive crowds to watch a firework extravaganza on the bridge. This had been preceded by Concorde making its last ever flight over the bridge in 2003 and the Olympic torch relay crossing over the bridge in 2012. One of the current maintenance engineering teams said on the television that while a modern bridge would be expected to last some 120 years, Brunel's structure was so well constructed and has been so well maintained that it is nearly as good as the day it was opened in 1864 and could well last for another 150 years!

I proposed in chapter 1 that bridges are generally a positive, connecting feature in society, with the notable exception of bridges built specifically for defence. However, very sadly people sometimes use bridges like Brunel's to make attempts on their own lives as had happened with a mother and her baby in the run up to the anniversary day. Surely in many cases such actions are very tragic escapist searches for some liberating sense of peace.

The Atlantic and Arctic convoys which I described in Chapter 3 had allowed Allied forces to be stationed in the UK as the plans for the liberation of Europe from the Nazis were put into place. On the night of June 5th 1944, Supreme Commander General Eisenhower's plan known as Operation Overlord, surely the most ambitious invasion plan of all time, was implemented in the shape of Operation Tonga, the code name given to the early airborne tasks of the British 6th Airborne Division to capture two strategically important bridges on the Caen canal and river Orne in Normandy. This was actually good forward planning intended to stop German counter attacks at Sword beach, Ouistreham, from the Eastern flank and from the Merveille gun battery in particular after the beach invasion of D-Day.

Pegasus bridge, situated outside Caen on the canal, is a bascule or balanced scale bridge. This means it is based on one span and is able to be swung perpendicularly to allow optimum canal traffic. Major John Howard led a group of 181 men in six Horsa gliders in the attempt to capture the two bridges.

As Sue and I stood reflectively in the meadow right next to Pegasus, it was starkly obvious how dangerous this had been, and had cost the lives of two of the men, Lieutenant Den Brotheridge and Lance-Corporal Fred Greenhalgh. Yet the gliders had found their target and landed in the complete dark, avoiding ponds and fields which as you know had been "staked" and topped with mines to deter landing attempts, and had landed with pinpoint accuracy in the first case within 50 yards of Pegasus bridge.

In fact the Germans were taken completely by surprise and the bridge was taken within 10 minutes. Horsa bridge, as the river Orne bridge became known, was captured swiftly afterwards. Parachute forces later backed up these forward glider troops. An excellent museum now contains the original bridge which was moved there and a replica placed over the Canal de Caen in 1994. Café Gondree, which was possibly the first French house liberated, still stands next to Pegasus and Arlette Gondree, the current owner, was only a child living there on D-Day.

It is exceptionally poignant to me that the bridge over the canal de Caen was renamed Pegasus, the name of one of the most well-known and inspirational Greek mythological animals…a pure white flying divine stallion. I cannot conceive of a more appropriate name to celebrate the memory of these courageous airborne heroes.

At the end of the war came the race across France and Germany to liberate Berlin, German's capital city. After the war, the Berlin Wall was constructed by the East German authorities starting in 1961, although for the first four or five years it was largely wire fence. I have already talked about the "Zonengrenze" or zoned border fence at Wittingen near where I was living and teaching in 1973. The Berlin Wall separated Soviet-occupied East Berlin, basically run under a Marxist/Leninist dictatorship style, from West Berlin which was run in a Western/Capitalist democratic style. Those in the East claimed they built the wall to stop fascists from the West trying to stop the development of a People's state in the Eastern sector. Those in the West claimed it was in simply to deter and eventually stop would-be escapees defecting.

There had been mass defections of East Germans prior to 1961, often including many of the educated classes in particular, people who left either for economic or political reasons or both. After 1961 some 5,000 escapes were attempted ending in the likely deaths of over 200 in Berlin. The museum near Checkpoint Charlie shows examples of clever ways people tried using all manner of escape methods from expanding suitcases to unusually-shaped and bespoke ladders and home-made aircraft or hot air balloons. Tunnels were frequently attempted. Some jumped out of apartment blocks in the early phases before those buildings near the fence or eventually the concrete walls were evacuated and boarded or gutted. Some tried to swim across the Spree canal.

The Wall stretched 96 miles around West Berlin, with 66 miles of concrete at its peak built to a height of 12 feet in about 45,000 sections. Once a second wall had been built inside the first in the Eastern sector, clear areas of "no go" territory among the death strips of mines and guard towers allowed potential escapees to be spotted and dealt with. Border guards often left the wounded or dying to bleed to death and it was largely impossible to help them as the East German border guards were ordered to fire.

Travel around Germany became difficult if not impossible. Not only could most East Germans no longer visit relatives in the West but many families became separated completely. There were indeed a number of official crossing points, nine of them in fact. But this was more a case of letting visitors from the West in. I mentioned that as a student teacher I was unable to visit the divided Berlin. Crossings were heavily patrolled and monitored by the East German border guards. Checkpoint Charlie was well known. When I visited the City many years later, someone directed me to a wonderful café nearby which serves many of the local police today with "Bratkartoffeln", beautiful roasted potatoes usually eaten in German custom with fried eggs and/ or "Schinken" (ham).

A few (four if I remember correctly) main Autobahn routes into the City were viable, one of which was near Braunschweig (Brunswick) and this would have been the one for me had I been able to get papers to visit West Berlin in 1973. Some rail routes were also possible. The underground system was also split between East and West. This involved some stations closing.

In 1963 John F.Kennedy famously visited West Berlin and gave his memorable "Ich bin ein Berliner" ("I am a Berliner") speech to a large crowd to show his empathy and support for the West Berliners who included American citizens.

Whilst the borders were strictly controlled through the 1970s and most of the 1980s, in 1989 the start of the wall's demise really came about with the symbolic escape of several thousand East German holidaymakers from Eastern bloc Hungary into Austria. Similar things happened in the former Czechoslovakia.

Demonstrations (known as the Peaceful Revolution) in East Germany led to Erich Honiker resigning. He had been in power from the early 1970s. In due course, not only was it possible to exit to the West via Hungary and Czechoslovakia, but also through some limited checkpoints even in Berlin itself. Due to an error in communication, it was transmitted on television one night that the borders were in fact open to anyone.

Mass gatherings of East Germans at the Berlin Wall and its more liberal checkpoints in particular took place very quickly. The East German guards became massively outnumbered and since no-one in office would take personal responsibility for a mass restraint exercise which would very likely have involved killing many of those gathered in order to stop the thing escalating, the guards opened the checkpoints and people started tearing the walls down and celebrating their new found freedom. I have not been back to the Lüneburg heath area since the end of the wall but I often wonder how those divided communities, where the fence literally split a village, must have tried to put their families back together again.

In November 2014, in order to mark the 25th anniversary of the fall of the Wall, a stunning Lichtgrenze or wall of light(s) was created using 8,000 luminous white balloons watched by over 300,000 people. Some of these tracked remnants of the Wall but in most places the balloons traced the original path of part of the wall in a 15 kilometre installation. Commemorative plaques with notable events from the history of the wall were placed exhibition-style along the Lichtgrenze. Angela Merkel the German Chancellor believed it offered hope to people where freedom and human rights had been threatened.

The Wirtschaftswunder (economic miracle) that took place after the war was due in part to the floods of dollars from the Americans contributing to the reconstruction of the German infrastructure and economy. German Chancellor Konrad Adenauer led a spectacular period of economic growth, building Germany up into one of the leading European nations. Over 25 years, it probably cost over 2 trillion euros. It is easy to see how the East German economy prior to reunification was very weak when you consider that GDP in the reunited Germany only increased from 1.7 (all West German) to 1.9 trillion after reunification.

Back in 1953, liberation had also been a key theme to be represented in the form of a bridge at the conclusion of the three year Korean War. Freedom Bridge was built over the River Imjin and brought home over 12,000 South Korean prisoners of war. This bridge was moved to Imjingak memorial park in 1972. There it is possible to see, on a guided tour, a loco-motive engine recovered from the demilitarised zone with over a thousand bullet holes and bent wheels from the ferocity of the war, along with a wall full of messages calling for reunification. During this conflict the Glori-ous Glosters, as they were known, the 1st Batallion of the 29th Independent Infantry, had performed their heroic stand on the Imjin River during the battle for Seoul when in 1951 around 650 of their Regiment had to face an entire Divison of some 10,000 Chinese soldiers and 622 Glosters died or were taken captive.

A few years later in 1965, the Edmund Pettus Bridge in Selma, Alabama in the USA, became the subject of a protest and conflict over freedom. Named after Edmund Winston Pettus, a former Confederate general, and built in 1940, this bridge was on the civil rights protest route from Selma to Montgomery. It was the venue for the so-called "Bloody Sunday" con-flict on March 7th 1965 when 600 civil rights demonstrators attempting to march peacefully to Montgomery after the shooting of Jimmie Lee Jackson were attacked by troops and police. Over 50 were hospitalized. Television ensured wide publicity in the USA.

Black voters had been harassed and intimidated as they went to regis-ter to vote that year. As a result of the march, Martin Luther King, torn between the need for pacifism and the need to make progress towards a change in legislation, himself called for civil rights supporters to come to Selma for a second peaceful march on "Turnaround Tuesday" April 9th, at which King avoided inciting conflict by getting the march to turn round short of the bridge. The pressure of a third peaceful march on March 21st led to the Voting Rights Act being passed in early August which then made it illegal to discriminate on voting practices.

The Bosphorus Bridge of 1973, which I was delighted to cross during a holiday to Istanbul in 2014, was designed by British engineers Sir Gilbert Roberts and William Brown who had an enviable track record with designs for the Humber, Severn and Forth Road bridges. It is one of two suspension bridges which cross over the Bosphorus, an iconic strait of water separating Europe and Asia. The place where East meets West. At just over 5,000 feet long, the Bosphorus Bridge stands 210 feet above sea level.

Historically, the idea of a bridge linking East with West had always been popular. King Darius of Persia had a pontoon bridge built across the Bosphorus in 513BC to afford him a stronger strategic position in the Balkans. By 1973, 35 engineers supported by a team of 400 workers had contributed to the modern Bosphorus Bridge. When fully loaded the bridge is supposed to sag nearly three feet! Toll fees are paid from Europe into Asia though not on the return journey. Plans are currently being debated for a 3rd bridge over the Bosphorus but there is considerable controversy over traffic levels and additional pollution in Istanbul.

In 2013, just outside St James' Church in Piccadilly, London, a replica of the wall surrounding Bethlehem was built. This wall was 26 feet high and made of concrete. Those who built it were not making any particular political statement or siding with either Israelis or Palestinians. The aim was simply to let people passing it think about the situation in the West Bank and especially around Bethlehem towards Christmas, and to reflect on what it meant to be on different sides of the wall.

If you recall the statement about not building walls until you are sure about what you are walling in and walling out, then you will appreciate that if walls are built to separate one community from another by one side, it can quickly cast shadows on the "others" who straight away become different as they are on the other or even "wrong" side of the wall. This seemed to be the case in Belfast during much of my childhood and I never really fully grasped the reasons for it at the time.

Near the Bethlehem Wall in London, poet Robert vas Dias wrote a thought-provoking piece called "Every Wall Has Two Sides"

"I didn't know I was on a side until a wall was built and then I knew I was on a side, the wrong side…"

Jennie Pollock in an article called "Rebuilder of ancient walls" puts forward an interesting argument.

"We are supposed to build bridges, not walls, aren't we? Or are we? I don't see that in the Bible. Yes, God tears down walls, and commands his people to do the same, but they are the walls that are barriers against Him and his glory – the Tower of Babel, the city of Sodom, the walls of Jericho… There are

at least as many instructions about building up walls – not to mention build-
ing the Temple. We ourselves are called living stones, Jesus is the capstone or
cornerstone, the end-point of the story is a Holy City. God tears down walls
when people start to put their trust in those walls rather than in him and his
provision, but walls in and of themselves are not wrong, and the word 'bridge'
is never even mentioned….. Perhaps the key is the context in which the walls
are built….. In other words, strong, secure walls only make sense – only do
what they are supposed to – in a world characterized by righteousness and
justice. And by contrast, it is only when the world is characterized by oppres-
sion and injustice that walls become negative things, things which oppress
and exclude rather than things which provide and protect".

I fully agree with the sentiments expressed here because up until now
my book has suggested that walls are things we really should be knocking
down and bridge are things we really should be putting up, and that is generally true because walls tend to divide and bridges tend to unite. But here
the sentiment is to build walls. However, they must be the right walls in the
right contexts, to shelter and protect and ultimate to liberate humanity, but
only when oppression has been relieved through justice.

Jennie concludes by saying that:

"Maybe then we will find that we ourselves have become the bricks in the
wall, with Christ as our firm foundation".

I would make the point that while she writes from a Christian perspective, and suggests what good Christians should be trying to achieve in following the example of Christ, any good individual, whether religious or
not, can earn the right to take their place as one of the bricks in this symbolic wall and maybe even become another of the keystones or capstones.
Whether this type of wall or a relationship bridge from Chapter 1 is the
easier (or harder) to build I do not claim to know. For both seem to me to
be as challenging as it gets in life. However for all of us there is abundant
hope, as you will read in my next and final chapter.

Chapter 6   The Power of the Creative

"There's a crack in everything, that's how the light gets in"
(Anthem: Leonard Cohen)

We often talk about the "ups" and "downs" of life. Life is such an incredible mixture of opposites. Whilst we would like life to be good all the time, we know this can never be so, and so we accustom ourselves to living through opposites, often extreme opposites, which can occur at any time and can totally change the delicate balance of our joys and our sorrows, our fears and our hopes within seconds.

We experience many opposites on our life journey: light and dark, win and loss, happiness and sadness, health and illness, fundamentalist and liberal. Sometimes these opposites are finely balanced, sometimes weighted heavily in one direction or the other. Just how we cope with these opposites depends on our understanding of people, the nature of the created world and its causal chain (the linking of causes and effects in the world), and for some an understanding of what is often referred to as the Divine.

My only brother Mike who lived in the Isle of Man passed away unexpectedly at the age of 78 just before Christmas, and this to some extent stopped me in my tracks as the funeral was in early January and I could not devote any real attention to finishing these chapters during that period for obvious reasons. In order to get from Ronaldsway airport to Douglas where he lived and ran the local yacht club for some years, it is necessary to pass over the Fairy Bridge. Locals are highly respectful of ensuring that visitors are encouraged to respect the fairies and to say good morning to them. I have never met any taxi driver there who acted otherwise.

I contend that the power of the creative is important. Whether or not you choose to go with the legend is up to you as you drive across Fairy Bridge, and indeed some might argue that such actions as I have described above are merely superstition and yet I can't help feeling drawn into a sense of respect for local customs and rituals. Perhaps that is the Religious Educator in me, but one could rightly ask whether the world might not have already been a much better and more coherent place had the Imperialist world considered the local beliefs and practices of indigenous peoples with a great deal more care and respect in previous times. I allude especially to the genocides in places like North America.

In the song "Anthem" by Canadian philosopher/songwriter Leonard Cohen, the suggestion is that our life situation does not allow for perfection, sadly not in any sphere of life, much as we try to achieve it (which of course is an excellent thing to try to do). Not only is life not perfect but there is a crack in everything, any kind of construction, real or symbolic, whether in something we make or in something we do or just in how we are. Some liken this to a small flaw in the (otherwise) flawless diamond that we are. However, the good thing is that the crack is where the light gets in.

The "brokenness" (remember the potter's house?) of constructed objects, and more crucially of human beings, is the very area where the light of true reconciliation and forgiveness, return and reconstruction can enter our world. For some this is the light of resurrection or The Resurrection, for others it is the light of reason and love. So the line of the song Anthem "Ring the bells that still can ring" is a call to each of us to not to be apathetic or resigned but to do what we can and contribute to the situations where the light is able to break through. We need to be creative to do this and there are plenty of examples to show just how much power we have in this huge creative challenge.

That power can be used for good or bad. If we are a "glass-is-half-empty" sort of people, we will see the downside to our challenges. If the "glass-is-half-full" we will look for the positive in most things we see and do. Take one of the newer crazes sweeping the country....drones. There are three main types to consider here, domestic, commercial and military drones. They will all play some part in our future for certain. I'll leave it to you to make your own mind up whether you are half full or half empty on this one, with some positive aspects first followed by some negatives.

Some of the positive uses of drones in domestic or commercial settings include aerial surveying of crops on farms, giving unique perspectives on sporting events, environmental monitoring of air quality and spying on illegal tipping, monitoring endangered species, transporting medicines in disaster areas, delivering medical equipment such as defibrillators to heart attack victims, monitoring and inspecting roads or bridges and pinpoint road blockages and delivering parcels to those in less accessible locations.

Some of the negatives include the possible invasion of personal privacy, for example on people in their own gardens, drones flying too near aircraft and being sucked into the air intake like a bird, the use of drones with lethal or non-lethal weapons, pinpoint assassinations of selected individuals, using a fleet of drones to conduct surveillance on whole towns or even cities or maintaining surveillance modes longer than military satellites.

I have not put these in any real order but there is certainly much food for thought. In thinking about walls and bridges, drones could even become bridges between people in some of the different ways I have described and could overfly walls for either good or evil purposes. We can be amazingly creative, but are we going to be a people bringing darkness or a people bringing light? The power of the creative should be seen in our attempts to live more simply. In Candide, French philosopher Voltaire writes "Il faut cultiver notre jardin" (we should cultivate our garden) which I take to mean living simply, touching the earth lightly and doing our bit for humanity, trying to improve everyone's standard of life and aiming to remove social injustice from the planet wherever possible. Some task indeed.

Catholics will be pleased to see that in this respect the current Pope Francis has tried to set an example to the world by getting rid of some of the trappings of luxury and keeping things as simple as it is possible for a Pope to do.

It is no coincidence that the term Pontifex is used of the Pope. The term can be translated as "bridge–builder" and that is certainly one of the things this current Pope and previous Pope John Paul 2 have been aware of trying to do, Pope John Paul 2 by his extensive programs of visits to the Churches throughout the world but also by developing interfaith dialogue among the major world religions. Here the attempts were to find common ground and celebrate it rather than concentrate on difference. Some might argue this was well overdue from the Catholic Church but the larger organisation is often slow to change and the Catholic Church believes itself to be a unique protector of Christ's teachings on earth following Jesus's symbolic giving of the keys of the kingdom of heaven to Peter as the first Pope.

With the Vatican fully aware of the need to communicate the Gospel message in the modern world, a Tweet from Pontifex on the subject of the family unit, arguably one of the most crucial basic building blocks of society in this and every other century, highlights one of the Pope's key hopes for spreading the Gospel "*That parents may be true evangelizers, passing on to their children the precious gift of faith*".

Pope Francis has gained a reputation for trying to develop the interfaith dialogue which Pope John Paul 2 was so keen to re-establish and his visits since 2013 fully reflect this. Francis visited Amman, Bethlehem and Jerusalem during 2014. During that tour he met with Patriarch Bartholomew I to develop inter-faith dialogue with the Orthodox Church. It was the first time in Catholic Church history that a Pope has invited a Jewish rabbi and an Islamic leader to an official delegation making its way to one of the world's holiest, and most contentious cities, Jerusalem, for worship in unison, and using a unified spiritual approach to master conflict.

Father Rifat Bader, director of the Vatican's media centre in Amman, argued that

"*Co-operation and friendship between Muslims and Christians alone can resolve problems and bring justice and peace to the world.*"

He suggested this is more than just tolerating other faiths, but is about friendship and service rather than simply about talking.

This of course is difficult. Archbishop Rajic believes that any hope of a lasting result from interfaith dialogue is about basic local leadership in schools, churches, mosques and synagogues - and the willingness and desire to continue to learn about one's own faith as well as about the other faiths.

In South Korea, Pope Francis's five day visit ended with a Mass for peace and reconciliation of the Korean peninsula. In Albania, Francis indicated he hoped his visit would be a stepping stone to unity between the various religions by establishing a national unity government to include Muslims and Orthodox and Catholic Christians. In France, he spoke to the European Parliament and the Council of Europe over topics such as the proper treatment of immigrants arriving illegally in Europe and improved conditions for workers. Finally in Turkey, he met with President Erdoğan and gave a speech urging interfaith dialogue to counter fanaticism and fundamentalism.

Pope Francis visited Sri Lanka and the Philippines in January 2015. He begged the multi-ethnic, multi-religious population to promote

"*human dignity, respect for human rights and the full inclusion of each member of society.*"

"I hope that interreligious and ecumenical cooperation will demonstrate that men and women do not have to forsake their identity, whether ethnic or religious, in order to live in harmony," he said.

There is clearly hope but the situation is difficult in places. Hard-line Buddhist groups and militants have on occasions attacked Hindu temples, Muslim mosques and Christian churches, particularly Evangelical churches. This is relatively new in Sri Lanka. Some groups had destroyed mosques and churches in 2013 as security forces stood by, the U.S. State Department's International Religious Freedom Report says. In 2012 and 2013, more than 100 attacks were recorded, according to Christian group Aid to the Church in Need. The need for not only interfaith dialogue but interfaith service and action is therefore essential if progress is to be made in this key area.

When it comes to building creative, modern bridges designed to impress, there are many exciting examples to be viewed around the world. Toxel.com features some of these. Among my personal favourites are the Aiola island bridge at Graz in Austria designed by Vito Acconci which incorporates a sunbathing area and coffee house, the beautiful Langkawi Sky Bridge in Malaysia, 700 metre above sea level and built as a panoramic walkway over mountain tops, the Octavia Frias de Oliveira bridge in São Paulo, Brazil, unusually built in an x-shaped style, an unconventional Rolling bridge near Paddington which curls back on itself, and a Swiss Traversina footbridge, with a unique staircase construction, employing graphic statics (using a Cremona diagram) to work out the cable tensions and variable geometry. As this bridge is built with a staircase effect running up the side of a steep gorge, and with only footpaths to work with during the build, the ingenuity of the construction is very evident. The very impressive results were achieved courtesy of the combination of a cable crane and a helicopter.

When it comes to building creative bridges among peoples, it would seem that Harald Bluetooth had a lasting reputation. Probably born around 920AD he ruled as King of Denmark from around 958AD until about 986AD. Some say he ruled as King of Norway and part of Sweden too from around 970AD. His conversion to Christianity is an interesting though debated one. One of the more popular accounts suggests that a priest named Poppa when asked by Harald to prove his faith carried a large piece of heated ironwork without being burned by it.

It is often argued that he proved himself to be very adept at getting others to connect with each other and work together. Indeed he was credited with uniting the disparate and dissonant tribes of Denmark under his rule. He is also reputed to have had the oldest bridge in southern Scandinavia built.

He is broadly viewed as wise and fair King. This is one of the main reasons why Bluetooth was chosen to represent the wireless technology data communications exchange system we know today invented in 1994 by Eriksson. In the Bluetooth communications system, protocols are united under one common standard.

The name Bluetooth is often assumed to be the result of Harald having a readily visible dark (bad?) tooth, although others suggest it was more to do with the wealthy blue regalia he wore or to do with the hue of his skin. The Bluetooth logo consists of the Scandinavian Younger Futhark runes of his initials, H and B.

Human nature is a wonderful mixture. Although we have our very dark side, demonstrated through the vicissitudes of history, and by some of the examples I have used to date, we are also capable of extraordinary altruism. Nowhere is this more apparent than in the field of charity. Looking at the Charities Commission, the top 10 charities in 2015 include some of the well-known names such as Save the Children, Cancer Research and Oxfam. The total annual income from these three alone is over £1 million. There are some 180,000 charities in England and Wales with a combined income of nearly £65 billion and spends of nearly £62 billion, a good sign showing that monies are being turned over. In this sector, there are over 900,000 employed and nearly 4 million volunteers.

I have noted how these charities grab the attention of young people and that they are keen to support them where there is a story relevant to their own lives. For example, at the Race for Life it is always moving to see the tributes and causes written on the t-shirts of many of the participants. My son Chris raised a substantial amount of money by fun run sponsorship to support the Stroke Association following my father-in-law suffering a severe stroke. Rob has done similar good things in supporting fun runs in the South West.

Cafod, the Catholic Agency for Overseas Development, previously known as the Catholic Fund for Overseas Development, is the Catholic Church's aid agency for England and Wales. Cafod is part of Caritas International and working in 160 countries to relieve poverty and suffering in developing countries. With an income of over £50 million, it is funded through the Catholic Church community in England and Wales, by public donations and partly by HM Government as part of DEC (Disasters Emergency Committee). Cafod takes a lead in the post-2015 Sustainable Development Goals process.

Founded in 1962, CAFOD provides both short term aid and long-term sustainable development, responds to emergencies, raises awareness and speaks out on behalf of the poor. It does all this in the spirit of the values of the Christian Gospel as Jesus's message was to bring Good News to the poor. This excellent aid agency, along with the other well-known and respected members of DEC, is always looking for creative and challenging ways to inspire and enthuse young and old alike to bridge the gap between rich and poor.

This is a much wider brief than merely offering emergency aid, although this is an important part of the role too, because Cafod seeks to end practices which discriminate and which are an obstacle to fair trading, trying to educate the developed world to respect the intrinsic dignity and human rights of each individual. It aims to help communities be self-supporting through its longer term project such as literacy programs, health care interventions and water engineering projects. It challenges Governments on issues of social justice policies. Our school, under the inspiration of one truly outstanding and unbelievably committed member of staff, raised huge amounts of money for Cafod over the years and it was a huge privilege to be part of this.

The BBC's Children in Need has raised, since its inception in 1980, over £600 million for projects designed to improve the lives of children with disability or difficult circumstances in the UK. Along with Sport Relief and Comic Relief (Red Nose Day) it runs highly effective annual telethons to boost its income stream and to educate the general public to be more altruistic where need is apparent. Using celebrity singers, dancers and actors, it provides material which is deemed both entertaining and reflective. Its mascot "Pudsey Bear", with its famous bandana over one eye, on some occasions wearing a sad expression, seems wholly appropriate with the theme of helping children and had endeared itself to the nation over the years. On many occasions a theme song has been used and CDs or downloads purchased by the public to raise extra funds. On one occasion the theme song was "Love can build a bridge".

Fun-running to raise money for charity has been a hugely positive innovation to show how love continues to build some amazing bridges. I do not wish to paint a picture that shows running for charity or indeed any distance running to be easy for in many cases it is exactly the opposite. In marathon running, for example, there is the famous "Wall" which many runners hit at around 20 miles.

It felt like an elephant had jumped out of a tree onto my shoulders and was making me carry it the rest of the way in."—Dick Beardsley, speaking of hitting "The Wall" at the second marathon of his career, the 1977 City of Lakes Marathon.

"*I didn't want to talk much. And when I'm not talking, you know I'm hurting.*"—Don Frichtl, a runner who encountered "The Wall" somewhere after mile 21 of the 2002 Chicago Marathon.

"*At around mile 23, I was beginning to feel like the anchor was out.*"— George Ringler who was speaking of his 1991 Lake County Marathon.

Those who have experienced "the wall" (including unfortunately yours truly!) often say it is like having your legs filled with lead weights. What is basically happening is that your body is running out of energy.

Overcoming the wall is not easy and demands courage, doggedness and a strong will to succeed in finishing the race. The trick, as is well known now of course, is not to start your race too quickly so that you do not burn off too much glucose too early, and to keep well hydrated during the entire course of the race combined with a carbohydrate-heavy diet to build energy and stamina and delay glycogen usage. Taking regular readings at various points in the race makes sense but it is probably not advisable to do it all the time.

Human nature, then, can boast many examples of working towards social justice and ensuring dignity and respect particularly when it considers the needs of others and when good will, intention and motive "shine forth like a precious jewel" as philosopher Kant claims. It is, at the same time, able to laugh at itself and this is no bad thing. Satire, as long as it does not degenerate into pure sarcasm all the time, allows us not to take things too seriously all the time and can be highly creative and amusing. To satire add being creative (admittedly at times subversively) with walls and bridges and you inevitably come up with Banksy.

Reputed to be from Bristol, and a former member of the Cathedral Choir School, Banksy's satirical artistic style combines a variety of street, underground and graffiti techniques mostly achieved through a unique sten-cilled effect. Originally the work was purely mused at by the passing public as they gazed at some of his work around Bristol, but as his reputation spread the nature of the work became much more iconic. This led to some attempting to deface his pictures and others trying to buy them, if neces-sary by removing the door, wall or whatever background feature the image was placed upon.

Many of his works mock the established authorities, capitalism or war-fare. In 2005 he visited Israel and nine images appeared on the Israeli West Bank Wall. Some pictures are simply that, although others include com-ments or slogans.

Controversy reached new heights when a remarkable piece entitled Mobile Lovers appeared on a door outside Broad Plain Boys Club in Bris-tol. The piece shows two adults looking at their mobiles over each other's shoulders as they embrace each other. A disagreement over ownership took place with the council ending up with Banksy allegedly giving the Club the work and it being sold privately for over £400,000. This proba-bly saved the club, together with several others with whom the proceeds would be shared, from financial disaster.

The other piece which courted much controversy was the piece on a wall in Cheltenham (home to GCHQ, the Government's communications and intelligence centre) featuring three spies apparently tapping the calls at a phone booth. Much had been debated at the time in the press and in Parliament about surveillance techniques exacerbated largely by whistle blower Edward Snowden's revelations. Bidding battles have taken place over the piece at the same time as various attempts have been made to vandalise it, following which the work has been screened off for its own protection. Banksy's work "One Nation under CCTV" is probably among the most controversial with Westminster City Council in 2008 stating that it was graffiti and would be painted over. They argued that Banksy had no more right to paint graffiti than a child.

There are of course many attempts at uniting the world through, for example, sport with the Olympic Games and through World Cups which are scheduled to take place every few years so that they are regarded as a special event which of course involves monumental amounts of organi-zation. However some creative ideas are a lot simpler and on a smaller basis whilst retaining the theme of bringing people together by celebrating things they have in common rather than things which divide. Continuing with the Bristol creative theme, it is good to see other artists who are trying in their own ways to provide such creative opportunities across the globe, itself forming some kind of unifying bridge across the world. Take Luke Jerram's artistic project "Play me I'm Yours". It appears that over 1,300 pianos have been rescued or recycled in one way or another and have been placed in public areas within more than 40 cities worldwide. Areas where these pianos have been installed include parks, railway stations, hotel lobbies, markets and bus shelters. Anyone from the public is invited to use them and play whatever they wish. Many of the pianos have been decorated and personalized. The idea is that the public in a sense take responsibility for a part of their city environment.

'The idea for "Play Me, I'm Yours" came from visiting my local launderette. I saw the same people there each weekend and yet no one talked to one another. I suddenly realised that within a city, there must be hundreds of these invisible communities, regularly spending time with one another in silence. Placing a piano into the space was my solution to this problem, acting as a catalyst for conversation and changing the dynamics of a space.'

(Luke Jerram)

This project has thrown up some heart-warming stories about players who do not have access normally to pianos being able to let their talent be shown in public. In some larger cities, pianos become available in quite large numbers as people move on or change their hobbies and interests, and Jerram has had plenty of examples to ship around the globe.

"...a simple concept that brings out the best in people. It reminds us of the strange and beautiful things that can happen in everyday life. I had one of the most memorable experiences of my life playing beneath the Sacre Coeur, Paris, on an old upright piano for a few hundred people".

Jamie Cullum on Paris Street Pianos

The public are invited to share pictures, videos, sound bites and stories linked to their playing. This enables the sharing of the project at a local as well as at a global level. What nicer or more positive way of connecting communities through one simple creative idea?

Teaching A-Level Ethics has always proved challenging both to the students and to myself, and no topic more so than that of Genetic Engineering. As I prepare to step aside from the syllabus I have taught for over 20 years, and which has developed greatly in that time, I feel a deep sense of loss at the thought that I will play no further part in the classroom discussing topics like therapeutic cloning. This is an exciting, challenging but brilliantly creative area of medical development in the use of stem cells, among others, in attempts to repair and replace worn or damaged body parts or cells or to select cells beneficially to customize our body design following the successful project to map the human genome at the turn of the century. The possiblity of finding solutions to debilitating diseases such as Alzheimers or Parkinsons thrills me, even though I am fully aware as an ethicist that there are always at least two sides to any debate about the use of the radical and costly technologies needed to do this.

Just over ten years ago there was a TV programme made which was a spoof court case set in 2014 called "If cloning could cure us". I used this programme consistently over those ten years in my classroom and it has always fascinated students and forced them to think critically. It featured the case of a climber who had broken his back in a fall and the various discussions among many stakeholders about the ethics of a cure involving the use of stem cells. A female Doctor was accused in court of illegally experimenting on embryos over 14 days old (the primitive streak) in order to use the harvested stem cells to repair the damage in the climber's spine.

My A-Level groups worked out that a very broad range of stakeholders here included scientists, bioethicists, fertilisation and embryology specialists, theologians and philosophers, medical researchers, egg donors, lawyers, patent/licence holders, pharmaceutical companies, the Government, lawyers and the police. This meant that not only the procedures themselves but their ethical justification was immensely complex. A selection of these stakeholders featured in the programme and at key points they would add their own comments and perceptions.

At the end of the programme, the opportunity was given to a TV audience to phone in with their verdict. Was the Doctor guilty or was she as she claimed simply trying to use the science in the interest of her patient who had become severely depressed with his condition? One of the commentators was Professor Geoff Raisman, acknowledged as a specialist in Neuroscience and Neural Regeneration in particular. I always hoped that the sort of technology featured in the film could one day become reality but in an ethically acceptable way.

When 2014 came round, I was totally amazed to find that no less than Geoffrey Raisman himself had played the key research role in the first-of-its-kind project repairing a badly severed spinal chord using Olfactory Ensheathing Cells and strips of tissue from the patient's leg to form a bridge repair over the damaged area.

Darek Fidyka, a Bulgarian man who was paralysed after a knife attack in 2010, is now able to walk using a frame. Attacked with a knife and repeatedly stabbed in the back over a potential infidelity, Darek had a small amount of scar tissue left but this was enough for the surgeon to work with. Over all those years, Professor Raisman had been researching the possibility of spinal chord regeneration using body cells and latterly had been working from University College London collaboratively with a Polish team assembled and headed by Dr Paweł Tabakow under Professor Włodzimierz Jarmundowicz at the Department of Neurosurgery at Wrocław Medical University.

The procedure involved the removal of one of Darek Fidyka's olfactory bulbs, the nasal cells forming part of the body's senses of smell, growing them on in a laboratory. These particular cells are highly suited to this type of procedure as they one of the few types of cell in the body that constantly renew themselves, and their usual role is to repair nasal nerve damage. The cells were injected (100 micro injections) into the patient's spine on either side of the spinal damage and strips of nerve tissue from his ankle were placed across the gap, in a long and complex operation.

The Olfactory Ensheathing cells provided a path to enable fibres above and below the injury to reconnect, using the nerve grafts to bridge the gap in the cord. The tissue was his, so there was very little fear of cell rejection. Since the operation, scans revealed the gap had closed up and feeling started to return to a patient who had been given virtually no chance of ever walking again. With physiotherapy and care, Darek has started to make good progress towards walking again two years after the operation. When I contacted him, Professor Raisman sent me some of his notes in which he suggests that:

"We believe that this procedure is the breakthrough which, as it is further developed, will result in a historic change in the currently hopeless outlook for people disabled by spinal cord injury."

"The combination of OECs and nerve strips was carried out on the left of

the spinal injury. The pattern of recovery was that muscle control reappeared first in the left leg and sensation in the right. This matches the normal routes taken by spinal nerve fibres. This pattern of recovery would be difficult to explain on other grounds than reconnection of severed fibres"

(Professor Raisman)

It is hoped to treat more patients in due course. Geoff Raisman argues for patience and caution as this is just the start but with the right will and backing of the various stakeholders it could be the start of a major break-through in treating paralysis. This is a truly remarkable prospect partic-ularly as there may be scope for treatment of other nerve systems in the body in addition to the spine and I cannot imagine a more positive type of bridge than this one!

For my final contribution, I would ask whether you know what is meant by an Einstein-Rosen bridge. Even if you are unfamiliar with that term, it is still likely you will be familiar with the term "Wormhole". Ever since the 1930s, scientists have debated the possible existence of areas of warped or curved "spacetime" which might create tunnels through space. If they were able to be used, it might theoretically be possible to travel across space and time to bridge the galaxies and solar systems we as yet know little or nothing about. We can think of a wormhole as a 2-D surface folded over to allow two "mouths" connected by a tube. There is no evidence for these from empirical facts or observations, but it is widely agreed that they form part of our scientific thinking on areas concerning relativity. Archibald Wheeler first used the terminology "wormhole" in the 1950s although many argue the concept had already been suggested by Hermann Weyl in the 1920s.

It is highly debateable as to whether wormholes known as Einstein-Rosen bridges or Schwarzschild wormholes are able to be crossed, or whether some sort of material would have to be employed to keep the wormhole open, perhaps with negative mass cosmic material, whatever that might look like, as Kip Thorne has suggested. In any event, this would be complex as if the opening was to close whilst crossing the wormhole survival would be rendered impossible.

I have tried, in these pages, to pull together my two themes, walls and bridges, describing and discussing just a few of the many examples of both which have been constructed on the planet over the centuries. I have tried to go beyond that though, and through philosophy, theology, history and science and personal anecdotes have attempted to encourage you to think about real and symbolic walls and bridges of different types. The research I undertook to do this has certainly provided me with food for thought and as always there is far more that could have been investigated and included.

As I said at the start, my intention was only to highlight some examples of walls and bridges which can shed some light on human nature. I have endeavoured, as planned, to end on a positive note for I believe we are and should be people of hope, whether we are religious or not. Hobbes may well have had a point in some of his key words used to describe human existence and yet to look negatively at life too often surely allows us to run the risk of missing its beauty and infinite possibilities.

As my brother Mike put it in his motivational e-book entitled "*Superfit at seventy and healthy at one hundred*" (and which I was proud to read out as part of my tribute speech at his funeral):

"*I could never understand how anyone could be bored with life. There is just so much to know, so much to do, so much to learn and so much to be interested in, that no one could possibly pack it all into one lifetime. Life is a wonderful thing. The more you put into it, the more you get out of it!*

From the earliest time I can remember, I have always had an enquiring mind, always wanted to know more about life, people, politics, history, geography, different cultures and beliefs"

I am already thinking about the physical structures I wish to visit next, but if all this has taught me anything at all it is that family, friends and forming altruistic relationships with others are among the most important things in life and it is surely in these areas that we must seek first to build symbolic bridges (and walls) of the right type that are every bit as real as the physical ones we continue to construct.

I would hope you agree.

Select Bibliography

Books

Beevor, Anthony, D-Day, Penguin, 2009

Bell, P.M.H, Twelve turning points of the Second World War Yale, UP, 2011

Campbell, J, The Hero with a thousand faces, New World Library, 3rd edit, 2008

Cruickshank, Dan, Bridges…Heroic Designs that Changed the World, Collins 2010

Graf,B Bridges that changed the world, Prestel, 2005

New Illustrated history of World War 2, David and Charles, 2005

McMahon, James, Making and Playing Marionettes, Harrop, 1957

Pixley, A, The Prisoner, Network, 2007

Powell, John Why am I afraid to love? Fount, 1967

Ruthven, Malise, Fundamentalism, OUP, 2004

Taylor, A.J.P and Mayer,S.L. History of World War 2, Octopus, 1974

Websites

en. wikipedia.org Fannie Mae

en. wikipedia.org Freddie Mac

www. sparknotes.com Frost's early poems "Mending Wall"

www.brantacam.co.uk About some Bridge Designers

https:// hbr. org.org/2011/06, Why a great individual is better than a good team by Jeff Stiebel

www.legendarydartmoor.co.uk Aspects of Dartmoor, Dartmoor Clapper bridges

www.heritagegateway.org.uk Exmoor National Park HER

47-178-1-PB.pdf Prison with Symbolic Walls

bigorangeslide.com/2009/09, Social alienation by Jon Finkelstein

en.wikipedia.org Battle of the Atlantic

www.history.co.uk Code breaking 09/1939 to 09/1945

www.history.co.uk Battle of the Atlantic 09/1939 to 09/1945

www.relevantmagazine.com   Why do we love Superheroes?
www.thewire.com /entertainment/2012/05, On the importance of having Superheroes by Jen Doll
https:// cuwhist.files.wordpress.com/2012/04, Batman crucified
en.wikipedia.org The American Monomyth
https:// answersingenesis.org/archaeology/The walls of Jericho
en.wikipedia.org Bryant G. Wood
https:// political ideology 1985.wordpress.com/2013/11/27, Mostar Bridge
en.theKotel.org What is the Western wall?
www.Kvetchingeditor.com/2009/01 Vespasian and the Western Wall
www.sharing.org Mesbahi, M, A discourse of isms and the principle of sharing.
www.forbes.com/sites/morganbrennan/2013 Billionaire Bunkers
www.democracyarsenal.org/2010/04 Israel's Cult of Securitism
en.wikipedia.org   Proposals for a Palestinian State
en.wikipedia.org Croat-Bosniak War
www.ecmi.de/Jemie/2012   An exploration of the Stari Most   S.Krishnamurthy
en. wikipedia.org   Stalag Luft 3
en.wikipedia.org   Pegasus Bridge
en.wikipedia.org   Berlin Wall
en.wikipedia.org   Europabrücke
en.wikipedia.org   Wormhole
www.thinktheology.co.uk /blog/article/Rebuilder of Ancient Walls
www.fiercelyalive.com/ blog/   Make Hummus not Walls
www.softhearthardfeet.blogspot.co.uk/2014/01   All They Draw is the Wall
en.wikipedia.org Bosphorus Bridge
www.highestbridges.com Europa Bridge
https:// orionmagazine.org The Nature of Walls by Jon Piasecki
www.gizmodo.com Some Good Things Drones can Actually Do
www.livescience.com 9 Totally Cool uses for Drones
www.marathonandbeyond.com Hitting "The Wall" by Sarah Latta
www.mindsparks.com Bridge to Freedom 1965
www.superfitatseventy.com
en.wikipedia.org Edmund Pettus Bridge
en.wikipedia.org   Imjingak
www.world-walk-about.com Korea's DMZ

en.wikipedia.org   Banksy

www.adventure.howstuffworks.com How hitting the Wall works by K Allen

www.guardian.com/notesandqueries/ Where does the computer term Bluetooth come from?

en.wikipedia.org Bluetooth

www.prgs.edu/content RAND National Security Research Division New Age of Terrorism Chapter 8 Jenkins, Brian

www.cafod.org.uk

www.charity-commission.gov.uk

www.bbcchildreninneed.co.uk

www.livewire.amnesty.org/2014/11/07 Walls and Bridges

www.spinalchord-symposium-brescia.it

www.toxel.com 10 Unusual and Creative Bridges